Words of Praise for Gordon Smith

'There's nothing ambiguous about the messages Gordon conveys … Hailed as Britain's most accurate medium.'
The Daily Mail

'Gordon's gift is to soothe the grief of the heartbroken, to give them hope.'
The Guardian

'Gordon Smith is down-to-earth about his heavenly talents.'
The Sunday Telegraph magazine

'Amazing.'
Time Out

'Utterly compelling'
Scotland on Sunday

'You don't meet men like Gordon Smith every day – he's the Psychic Barber who never needs to ask where you're going on holiday.'
The Scotsman

'Gordon's honest, gentle and humorous approach has deeply impressed me.'
Michelle Collins, actress

'The talent Gordon has been blessed with is something most of us can hardly believe, but to see and hear of the help he has given others in easing their pain is surely his greatest gift. He's also a reasonable barber!'
Ally McCoist, MBE, sporting personality

D0107545

The
Unbelievable
Truth

Also by Gordon Smith:
Spirit Messenger

Hay House Titles of Related Interest:

Books

Adventures of a Psychic, by Sylvia Browne

Angel Medicine, by Doreen Virtue, Ph.D.

Born Knowing, by John Holland

Chakra Clearing, by Doreen Virtue, Ph.D.

Conversations with the Other Side, by Sylvia Browne

Crossing Over, by John Edward

Diary of a Psychic, by Sonia Choquette

Contacting your Spirit Guide, by Sylvia Browne

Card Decks

Archangel Oracle Cards, by Doreen Virtue, Ph.D.

Healing with the Angels Oracle Cards, by Doreen Virtue, Ph.D.

Heart and Soul Cards, by Sylvia Browne

Messages from your Angels Oracle Cards, by Doreen Virtue, Ph.D.

All of the above are available at your local bookshop or may be ordered by visiting:
Hay House UK: www.hayhouse.co.uk
Hay House USA: www.hayhouse.com
Hay House Australia: www.hayhouse.com.au
Hay House South Africa: orders@psdprom.co.za

The
Unbelievable
Truth

Gordon Smith

HAY HOUSE

Australia • Canada • Hong Kong
South Africa • United Kingdom • United States

Published and distributed in the United Kingdom by:
Hay House UK, Ltd • Unit 62, Canalot Studios • 222 Kensal Rd, London W10 5BN
Tel: (44) 20 8962 1230 • Fax: (44) 20 8962 1239 • www.hayhouse.co.uk

Published and distributed in the United States of America by:
Hay House, Inc. • PO Box 5100 • Carlsbad • CA 92018-5100
Tel: (1) 760 431 7695 or (800) 654 5126 • Fax: (1) 760 431 6948 or (800) 650 5115
www.hayhouse.com

Published and distributed in Australia by:
Hay House Australia, Ltd • 18/36 Ralph St. • Alexandria NSW 2015
Tel: (61) 2 9669 4299 • Fax: (61) 2 9669 4144 • www.hayhouse.com.au

Published and distributed in the Republic of South Africa by:
Hay House SA (Pty), Ltd • P.O. Box 990 • Witkoppen 2068
Tel/Fax: (27) 11 706 6612 • orders@psdprom.co.za

Distributed in Canada by:
Raincoast • 9050 Shaughnessy St., Vancouver, B.C. V6P 6E5
Tel: (1) 604 323 7100 • Fax: (1) 604 323 2600

© Gordon Smith, 2004, 2005

Design: e-Digital Design
Edited by Lizzie Hutchins

A catalogue record for this book is available from the British Library.

ISBN 1-4019-0549-8 (paperback)

ISBN 1-4019-0359-2 (hardback)

Printed and bound in Great Britain by The Cromwell Press Ltd, Trowbridge, Wilts.

For my mother and father
and my family
and all those who have inspired me.

Contents

Acknowledgements   *x*

Introduction   *xi*

Chapter One   **Mediums and Psychics**   1

Chapter Two   **Life After Death**   33

Chapter Three   **Heaven and Hell**   55

Chapter Four   **Ghosts and Spirits**   73

Chapter Five   **Poltergeists and Hauntings**   95

Chapter Six   **Public Non-Reality**   117

Chapter Seven   **Altered States**   143

Chapter Eight   **Strands of Time**   173

Chapter Nine   **Reincarnation**   193

Chapter Ten   **Consciousness**   215

Further Reading   *239*

Acknowledgements

I would like to thank Meg, for providing me with the inspiration for this book, Jo for looking after me so well, and Michelle for her nurturing guidance. Thanks also to Reid and Leon for their vision and to the other Hay House girls for their hard work and constant support.

Ros, thank you for your support and more importantly your friendship.

Dronma, thanks for being you.

Tricia and Archie, thank you for your help and your wonderful stories.

My son Paul, thank you for your help and your patience!

And a special thank you to Lizzie for all her hard work and perseverance.

Introduction

It never ceases to amaze me how many people have questions about the so-called unexplained – questions about ghosts and miracles, reincarnation, life after death, out-of-body and near-death experiences. Subjects like these and many more have fascinated me since I was very young. Since childhood I have seen the spirits of people who have died. I had my first ever paranormal experience when I saw the spirit of someone close to our family shortly after his death. My mother's reaction was one of shock and horror. She forbade me from ever mentioning my encounters with the spirit people, yet later on I still ended up becoming a recognized medium.

Mediums have been giving evidence of spirit survival for many years, but this is just the first step in investigating the unseen world around us. Most people have encountered something strange at some point in their lives that has made them look differently at the world they live in. Some have witnessed spirits who have appeared to give warnings or messages to their loved ones. Others have heard children give accurate accounts of previous lives or have experienced miraculous healing or seen spirits or angels. One of the biggest questions I was left with when putting together some of the amazing stories in this book was why, if so many people have experienced so many supernatural occurrences, don't we hear more about them?

One reason is that there are so many myths and mysteries attached to the paranormal that many people don't know what to believe. I can understand this. I have been around the world of psychics, mediums and all sorts of so-called spiritual practitioners for almost half of my life and have experienced amazing phenomena, but even so, I certainly don't believe everything I have been exposed to and neither would I expect others to. Not everyone who claims to be psychic actually is. It is important to learn to see past the charade and find the truth, whatever that may be.

In *The Unbelievable Truth* I have attempted to shed some light on the dark corners where ignorance can breed fear. I have spent most of my life trying to convince people that there is life after death, yet the mediumship which I share with people is only one small part of the bigger picture of our continued life. Once we accept that our spirit will live on after death, then comes the question: what is it like in the afterlife? And where is the afterlife? Where do we go? Is there a Heaven and Hell and what qualifies you to go to one or the other?

What I have found is that to understand anything about the nature of the unseen world, you first have to try to understand your own nature – to become conscious of what you are in this life, where you've come from and where you are going to. It is in the learning about ourselves, about our consciousness, that we can overcome our fears and doubts and accept what once seemed beyond belief as normal, everyday, even reassuring. And then all of a sudden we realize that life is playing out as it should.

Many of the episodes in this book I have been directly involved with; others have been shared with me by those who have encountered unbelievable happenings and have allowed me to investigate them further. Many of these accounts may appear to be unbelievable, but I can assure you that they are all, to the best of my knowledge, the truth.

Writing this book has been one of the most enlightening journeys I have made on my spiritual path. I hope that you will have as much enjoyment reading it as I did writing it, but more than that, I sincerely hope that it helps you in your search for truth.

CHAPTER ONE

Mediums and Psychics

Mediums and Psychics

What does it mean to be a medium? What do I actually do? It is not always easy to explain. Saying I communicate with discarnate spirits who have gone on after physical death sounds strange to some people. What sort of messages are passed on? What convinces people that their loved ones really are communicating with them? I've often thought that a good way to explain the process would be to film someone before they came to see me and ask them to share their story and what they hoped to gain from the encounter.

In January 2004 that very thing happened during the filming of a BBC documentary in which a couple who had lost their son in a car accident the year before were brought to see me. The director of the film had not allowed me to have any prior knowledge of the couple at all, not even where they were being brought from. This should actually be standard practice, as the less the medium knows about a person, the more convincing the evidence they may receive from the spirit world. In this case, unknown to me the couple had been filmed for some time before our meeting.

On a cold February morning I was waiting in the library of the London Spiritual Mission, where the sitting was to take place. This is one of the most beautiful Spiritualist churches in the UK, where mediums from all over the country come to demonstrate their skills. Once the film crew decided they were ready to begin, a couple who I would imagine were in their forties were asked to sit down opposite me and I explained to them how the sitting would proceed. Normally, I 'tune into' the spirit world by asking the spirit people if they would like to come and contact their loved one, but this time even as I began to tell the couple how it might work I could hear the voice of a young man shouting the name 'Andrew' over and over in my ear. With this I knew I had a communicator from the spirit world.

I started by saying, 'There is a young man on the other side and he is asking for Andrew.'

Immediately the man answered, 'I'm Andrew.'

Then I heard another name. I turned to the woman and said, 'You must be Margareta.'

'No,' she answered, but then it changed and I told her, 'I'm sorry, he has changed it to Greta.' This time she smiled and said that was her name.

Their son was now communicating at high speed, often so fast that I had to slow him down, but this was characteristic of how he behaved in life, so his mother told me. He told me that his name was Nige, short for Nigel, and that he and his friend were together in the spirit world as they had both been involved in the same accident. He went on to ask after other family members, told me to tell his sister to go back to her studies and mentioned a Mr Trainer, who turned out to be her tutor at college. Then he asked me to mention Ilkley. This is where he had been brought up and where he had spent much of his time with his teenage friends.

Nige wanted to convince his family that he was still very much a part of their life. He asked me to ask his father why no one wearing his watch, which was at home in a blue box. His father said he wanted to, but hadn't got round to putting in the new battery that it needed. Then Nige told his mother that he had been with her that morning when she had picked up three letters from behind the front door and that he knew she had wanted to bring the large picture of him with her to the sitting, but instead she had picked it up, touched his face and put it back. He also said that she could feel his presence when she walked through the lane at the back of her house. All of this was accepted by Andrew and Greta.

Nige also asked me to tell them that he had been with them when they had gone to Ilkley Moor and stood on his very favourite large rock. The camera and sound men were shocked at this, as they had filmed the family walking on Ilkley Moor the previous day and Andrew had stood on his son's favourite rock and said that he would say that it was like standing on top of the world. At the close of the sitting the crew again got a bit spooked when young Nige asked me to tell them all that he and his friend were fine and that he really was standing on top of the world.

Afterwards Greta and Andrew told me how moved and uplifted they had been by the sitting. They felt that their son's personality had really shone through and their overwhelming impression had been that he really was communicating with them. They were absolutely amazed that his spirit had been with them when they had been filmed on the moors and that he had then been able to tell them about it through my mediumship.

An encounter like this may be able to provide people with enough evidence to convince them that their loved ones live on after death and so help heal their grief. As a medium, my main task is to help those who need to find hope and comfort at such times.

Delivering Messages...

One of the greatest mediums of the last century was my old friend Albert Best. So detailed were his messages that people would often appear bewildered by his knowledge of their loved ones' lives. He would talk to the unseen and receive answers as though it were all quite normal and would often tell me about his experiences, including private sittings with celebrities and politicians from all over the world.

There are so many unbelievable episodes of mediumship associated with Albert, but one stands out in my mind because of who it was that became convinced by the evidence he was able to pass on from the other side.

Rev. David Kennedy, a Church of Scotland minister, was sitting with his wife Ann as she lay dying in a hospital bed in Glasgow. She was only in her forties, but he knew that there was no cure for her illness and that she would be gone from him in a very short time. So frail was her body that he could not even hold her close to him, but so brave was her spirit that she reassured him that she would find a way to come back to him from beyond the grave. And even though it was against his religious belief, he agreed to look for her sign.

The death of his wife hit David very hard. He found life becoming increasingly difficult without her and his faith in God was being tested to its very limits. Remembering her vow to give him a sign that her spirit lived on, he went to visit a Spiritualist medium called Lexie Findletter. She gave him a message from woman called Ann who claimed to be his wife, but David's natural scepticism and religious conditioning would not allow him to accept it. However, as he got up to leave the room, Mrs Findletter said, 'Your wife is determined to communicate with you and she will find a way.'

A week after his meeting with the medium, David felt even worse. Had his wife really been trying to get a message through to him? What if he hadn't given her a proper chance? In despair, he said out loud to the empty room, 'Come on, Ann, give me a sign, something that no one could possibly know, please!'

He lay down on the sofa, feeling exhausted at the thought of the sermon he would have to prepare for his service later that day. The next thing he knew, he was being woken by the sound of the phone ringing loudly. Lifting his head from the arm of the sofa, he looked at the clock on the wall and started to panic as he realized he only had five minutes to prepare his sermon and find a clean minister's collar. Ignoring the phone, he fumbled around the room looking for old notes and trying to remember where his clean collars were. Still the phone rang. Eventually he grabbed the receiver and shouted angrily, 'Can I help you?'.

'Your wife Ann is with me,' said a voice. 'She tells me that your clean collars are in the bottom drawer of your wardrobe and the speech you prepared last year for this service is in the top drawer of your desk. Incidentally, my name is Albert Best. Goodbye.'

David was stunned. He remembered that he and his wife had met Albert some years earlier at a social gathering. People had been raving about him as a medium and out of the blue he had told Ann that her brother who had died during the Second World War was standing beside her. He had given a perfect description of him. But how did he know to phone at that moment with the exact information he needed? And how did he get the number?

David went about his business as best he could that evening. In the weeks that followed he set about finding Albert and putting his powers to the test. He found out that Ann had appeared to Albert in spirit form and had provided the information about the collars and the sermon and the phone number. As time passed, David learned that if he sent out a thought to his wife when he was alone in the house, within a short time Albert would be on the phone with the answer. Once he even said, 'Tell your bloody wife to stop bloomin' bothering me, it's the middle of the night!'. And so it was. David had forgotten how late it was when he had sent the thought to Ann and now it was past three o'clock in the morning.

This continued for over a year and I remember Albert telling me he would often get annoyed with Ann's frequent requests for him to call her husband. But the more he protested, the more strongly the visions of Ann appeared and more clearly she spoke to him. Albert knew that she felt she had some kind of mission to convince her husband of her survival. It was obvious that she was going to stay on his case until her work was done.

Messages from the other side were not part of Rev. Kennedy's own religious teaching, but the more he tried to reason them away, the more baffled he became. Finally he asked Ann to do one more thing to prove her survival and told her that this time he would accept it. He asked her to give him a message through Albert concerning something about herself of which he knew nothing and then to confirm it through a member of her own family. The next time Ann appeared to Albert, she simply asked him if he would tell her husband to call her sister and ask about the ballet shoes. When David did so, his sister-in-law was astounded that he knew of the private joke which had been a secret between her and her sister for many years.

This message finally convinced David. He was left with no choice but to accept that his wife's consciousness was still able to communicate with him after her physical death. What was also apparent was that in her new state she was aware of his thoughts and actions and would respond to them through a medium. Most people don't realize that when they send out a thought it might well be picked up and often answered by someone on the other side. In this case it was certainly clear that Ann's spirit was receiving all of the messages from her husband, but he needed a medium to pick up the messages from her. So using a medium ultimately helped him to get over his loss and get on with his life, comforted by the knowledge that his wife's consciousness had survived. This to me is the reason why mediums are given such a gift.

After much thought and investigation into his experiences, David decided to write his story, which later became a book called *A Venture into Immortality*.

Incidentally, Albert Best worked as a postman for most of his life – delivering messages is what he was good at!

Truths and Misconceptions about Mediums

There are so many misconceptions about mediums. As a working medium myself, I do feel it's important to reveal the truth about what mediums can't, don't or even won't do!

- *Mediums call up the dead.* On the contrary, the spirit people attract the attention of the particular medium they feel attuned to in order to contact their loved one.

- *Mediums go into funny trances, speak in funny accents and know the answers to every mystery from why Atlantis sank to why British tennis players are so bad.* The truth is that they don't.

- *Mediums are always post-menopausal overweight women or youngish gay men.* No, they come in all shapes and sizes.

- *Mediums always have Native American spirit guides.* There are lots of Native American guides, but they're probably only there to try to sort out some of the cowboys who call themselves mediums.

- *All mediums use crystal balls to look into the future.* A crystal ball is a psychic prop similar to tarot cards and rune stones. A medium should be able to make contact with the spirit world without the aid of such props.

- *Mediums can call up anyone you might want to talk to on the other side.* The truth is that mediums cannot demand to make contact with a particular spirit.

For example, if a fan of Elvis Presley went to a medium and wanted to make contact with their hero, the chances are nothing much would happen. If Mr Presley's daughter went for a sitting, however, then there would be a spiritual link between the two of them and maybe he would communicate with her. (But what am I thinking? Isn't Elvis still alive?!)

Mediums and Psychics

Many people seem to associate mediums with psychics who consult a crystal ball or tarot cards. The sad thing is, they could not be farther from the truth. All mediums are psychic, but not all psychics are mediums.

People who are psychic show many different skills, including the ability to pick up information about someone's past, present and even future. Some people can move objects using the power of their mind, others can read thoughts and others can heal the sick. All of these phenomena and more come under the psychic banner, because they are produced from a person's own psychic energy field and not from the spirit world.

Some psychics have used their powers in very positive ways. Some claim to have helped the police on murder cases, using psychometry to tune into an object or piece of clothing taken from a crime scene and give detailed information about the particular crime, often with great success. Others have just helped the police with their enquiries! It has also been said that psychics were used by the military during the Cold War as remote viewers. (Remote viewing is when a person uses their mind to see events at a great distance.)

Someone with true psychic awareness can certainly access notable events in a person's life just by looking at them. Normally these are events that are stored in the emotional databanks of the mind. The psychic picks up on the emotional turbulence and uses it to establish a link to the person's mind. Once they have such a link they can usually come up with what is currently giving the person problems and can offer guidance.

Faking Psychics

A good psychic may help someone through a difficult time in their life, but like all things of this nature, there are charlatans. It is all too easy to find a problem, offer a solution and maybe polish the ego along the way. Who wouldn't feel better after that? Check the emotions and the body language, throw in the usual generalities like births, deaths and marriages and you have a successful reading. Cloud the memory with some psychcbabble, using terms the client has never heard of before, then make them feel good before they leave and they'll rave to all of their friends about how good the reading was, if only because they have just been stung for 30 to 50 quid or more.

It may be fun to invite a psychic into your home to read for a group of friends, but do remember that they may do more harm than good. My watchwords are 'common sense'. If you feel the psychic is asking questions of you rather than making statements that are relevant to your life, then the chances are they are guessing.

I remember one poor man who came to see me after he had lost his wife and had been round a lot of psychics in an effort to contact her on the other side. He had found most of these people through advertisements in newspapers and magazines. All, it seemed, had charged him extortionate amounts of money for their services and there had not been so much as a whisper from his dear wife. One woman had said that his gay partner in the spirit realms was trying to contact him, while another had given him a message from a Great Aunt Fanny he didn't have. Most of these psychic practitioners claimed to be direct descendants of the famous psychic Gypsy Rose Lee. What was the old gypsy girl doing in that tent to have so many direct descendants?

Sadly, between them these people had taken so much money from this vulnerable man that he had gone deep into debt and was pawning items from his home just to get by. That was bad enough, but by now he was so confused by everything he had been told that he didn't know if he was coming or going. All I could do was try to bring some common sense back into his mind and steer him away from the psychic circus that trades on people in this state.

My old teacher in the Spiritualist church used to say of mediums and psychics who charged money for private sittings or readings that you could tell a good one by their charge. By that she meant that the best were mostly those who charged little or nothing for their gift.

Is There Anybody There?

A psychic makes no claim to contact spirits on the other side, but many psychics will stumble into situations where their awareness will expand like psychic radar and they will begin to detect spirit messages in the space around their sitter. Even in this type of incident, however, the psychic is not communicating directly with the discarnate spirit but is passing information that the spirit has tried to convey to their loved one and that has remained in their aura or electromagnetic field. Mediums, on the other hand, work from a stronger battery that boosts their signal further afield and enables them to pick up signals from the conscious minds of those who have gone on to the spirit world.

Although a medium's range reaches the spirit realms, it also covers the psychic energy field, so a medium can also pick up information psychically from a person. Even though I am a medium who gives messages from the spirit world, I very often sense what people close to me are thinking or feeling and on many occasions I see images of future events in their life. This happened to me often as a child, when my gift was more unrefined; it wasn't until I joined the development class in my local Spiritualist church that I began to understand the difference between my psychic abilities and my mediumship.

A development class is made up of people wishing to develop their mediumistic or psychic ability. Within the group or circle there is a leader who will remain fully conscious and aware while the rest of the group still their minds and go within to a state of silence. The collection of people emitting psychic energy all together leads to a much stronger battery of power and the power around each sitter will become very intense. The medium has to learn to focus their mind on this intense energy, as this is where the link with the spirit world is forged.

The best place to join one of these groups is a well-run Spiritualist church that is governed by one of the Spiritualist organizations. The Spiritualist religion began more than 100 years ago and has grown to have hundreds of churches around Great Britain and in many countries around the world. In the early days, mediums produced many different types of phenomena where the spirits not only communicated from the other side but would often materialize at séances. They could form in a physical way if the medium could produce a substance known as ectoplasm. This was often described as a whitish misty substance. It would be seen flowing out of the medium's body and would become dense enough to allow the spirits to mould it into their image. When fully materialized in this way, they could walk freely around the people gathered, pick out their friends or relatives and converse with them. This phenomenon was at its height in the Victorian era and throughout both world wars, when people were going to the other side *en masse*. Although many intelligent witnesses testified to having experienced it, it was often criticized because in order for the medium to produce ectoplasm, séances were held in the dark or in dim red light.

It would seem that with time, mediumship has refined and become more mental, in that nowadays mediums hear, see and sense spirit people rather than produce ectoplasm for them to materialize physically. Gone also are the days when Spiritualists would sit together, often around a large table, and hold hands while the leader or main medium would go into a trance in order to allow a highly evolved spirit to use their mind and body.

Spirit Guides

One thing that has not changed is that all mediums need to trust in a spirit guide or teacher. This is someone who will make themselves known to you early in your development and who will guide each step you take on your spiritual journey. I consider this type of link between a medium and spirit guide to be like getting to know yourself on a higher level. Through the eyes of your guide, you can see the world in a much more compassionate and spiritual way.

Before I joined the development group I had never heard of spirit guides, even though I had had experiences with spirit people since early childhood. But the idea that a teacher was going to give me lessons was interesting to say the least. 'If I have a spirit guide, then what will they teach me?' I used to ask. 'And anyway, why do I need one?'

The reason is that spirit guide is like a safety point in your mind, an image, sense or sound that allows you to journey through altered states of your own consciousness and beyond. Whenever things get too much or become too intense, you can call on your guide, a bit like a child calling to a parent when they feel lost.

Another important lesson I learned very early in this class was how to turn my gift on and, more importantly, how to switch it off. I feel very sorry for those who say they have no control over this. If I could not switch off my mediumship I dread to think what it would be like at the barber shop where I work. Can you imagine me asking a customer how he would like his hair cut, only to hear his mother or father in the spirit world saying, 'Cut it shorter, don't listen to him!'?

The thing with spirit guides is that some people take the idea in completely the wrong way. There are those who begin to live the type of life they imagine the guide lived and, even worse, start to relate to the guide like a best mate. I remember one woman telling me that she had to change all the soft furnishings in her living room because her Tibetan guide stopped coming through her when she had her curtains and cushions made from a Chinese fabric. Well I never!

Many mediums claim to have famous people as guides. In my early days in the development circle I heard many 'famous guides' channel through their new medium. As well as many saints and legends like Joan of Arc, John the Baptist and so on (and on), there would be the odd showstopper like Judy Garland, who came through a male medium and performed some of the more famous songs from her repertoire. I was also told once by the wife of a man who was developing trance mediumship that for several weeks her husband would get out of bed in the middle of the night wearing only his underpants and talk in the voice of Elvis Presley for half an hour. His wife was so confused that she was 'all shook up'! Another medium claimed that her guide was the Beatles legend John Lennon. Can you *imagine*?

In my first three years in the development circle most of my experiences were of the type of mental mediumship that I had known from childhood, where I received messages in my mind. I had also watched some mediums going into a trance-like state. Sometimes a different voice would speak through them. On certain occasions it would be like really bad acting, but there were a few times when the most astounding spiritual lectures would be given.

I always hoped I would never experience this type of mediumship and until that point I never had. But then I had the most amazing experience. One night I was sitting as usual trying to be still, but as usual not a lot was happening and my mind started drifting. Then a light appeared in front of me, as if in the distance. Even though my eyes were shut tight, this light grew stronger and eventually I felt as if I was moving forward towards it. I felt illuminated and more alive than I had ever felt in my life. Then I seemed to fall asleep. Everything was peaceful until I heard a voice which seemed to break the amazing silence. I immediately opened my eyes to see everyone in the group staring at me with a look of shock on their faces.

The leader of the group, Mrs Primrose, now moved closer towards me and told me to take my time and come back slowly. As soon as she felt that I was fully awake she asked me to join her in her office away from everyone else. I felt quite bewildered by all of this, as all I had done was fall asleep after having a marvellous experience. But Mrs P. explained to me that my guide had spoken through me while I was in trance.

'While I was in what?!'

She went on to say that the particular spirit teacher who works with me had given her a very specific message that she alone could understand and that might save a child's life in the not too distant future. When she finished talking I was baffled, for I had no knowledge of speaking, let alone of someone else speaking through me.

There was another occurrence of this 'sleep trance mediumship' one week later. This one also involved a child whose life was in danger, but miraculously she lived. To this day I have no memory of what was said through me, but I do know that the words came from someone who wanted to save a child's life and I resolved that I would try to find and trust whoever that was. I say 'whoever' because mediums have more than one guide or teacher in the spirit world and different ones may come through from time to time in accordance with the situation that needs their help. That particular spirit teacher, I have come to learn, works with me whenever there is a need to help children. It's a bit like having different doctors who specialize in their own field.

Normally when I am about to begin a private sitting for someone, I simply send out a thought to the spirit guides who help me and within a second I become aware of who is helping me to communicate with the spirit world. This is one of the skills I have learned through years of meditation and the development of my awareness. Each spirit person who works with me has what I call their calling card, an indication of their identity that they 'impress' upon me. For example, one who is very small in height will make me feel as if my body is shrinking, while another who has a beard will identify himself by making me aware of lots of facial hair, and so on.

Being able to recognize the spirit guides and helpers I have built up trust in over the years allows me to establish my first contact with the spirit world. It is through my guides that I proceed with questions on behalf of my sitter, such as 'What was the person's name?' or 'When did they die?' and 'How did they die?'. During this process I may hear answers and pass them on to my sitter or I may feel sensations of illness or infirmity the spirit person lived through. Pictures may form in my mind of how the spirit person looked or of places where they lived or died. But most of what happens is sensed in feelings. All of these sensations are what Spiritualists call mental mediumship, because they are of a subjective nature and occur within the mind of the medium.

Give What You Get

When a medium has trust in their work it boosts their signal to the spirit world. Also, trusting the spirit world is important because sometimes what comes through seems so trivial and yet it could mean so much to your sitter. An instance of this happened to me recently and it proved to me that as a medium, mine is not to reason why, but just to give what I am getting.

A lady in her mid-forties was sitting in the chair opposite me and I was proceeding to give her the general rundown of how a private sitting should work when I heard the voice of a young man by my left ear, saying, 'Mum, I'm here'. I told the woman that she had a son in the spirit world and he was communicating already. Soon I had established his name and how he passed away and many features of his life. All seemed to be going well until his mother asked me if I could ask him about the code that they had made just before he died. I sent out the thought to her son and nothing came back.

The woman's face fell and I could tell that she had lost all faith in what I was doing. I tried to explain that her son was trying to give as much information about himself as possible in the half-hour that was allotted for his mother's sitting. I often look on a private sitting as the spirit person getting a chance to make a phone call. If you can imagine what you would say to your family in what might be a one-off call, I am sure it would not be very measured and concise conversation.

Finally, as the woman stood up to depart, I heard her son suddenly call out 'Clover!'. At this she stared at me, shocked.

Tears began to run down her cheeks. 'Oh my God!' she gasped. This was the code that they had agreed on. When the boy was very young he had found a four-leafed clover for his mother while on holiday in England. Then in his late teens he had been found to have cancer and it was while he was in hospital that he and his mother had agreed on the code that he would use if he could communicate with her after death.

It is quite amazing to watch the reaction on someone's face when a certain piece of evidence comes through from the other side. Sometimes just a word or phrase can put a light back on in a person's life. Usually it will be something simple but so meaningful that they are moved from belief to knowing.

Science and Sensibility

A word or phrase may convince a relative, but what of the scientists? For more than 100 years they have been investigating mediumship. During this time many intelligent people have witnessed many forms of mediumship and have been convinced that paranormal phenomena were occurring right in front of them. But were they? With all forms of mediumship, for every genuine exponent there would be a couple of charlatans just out to make money and play on the vulnerable. Back in the Victorian heyday of ectoplasm, I bet the sale of muslin and cheesecloth went soaring up.

In more recent times I have allowed myself to be tested by the Scottish Society for Psychical Research, which is based at the University of Glasgow. Over the course of seven years or so I have taken part in blind tests where I am not allowed to see the recipients of my messages or hear their replies to anything I say. I have also taken part in what they call double-blind tests, which involve me being asked to sit in one room while a group of people sits in another room. One of these people is chosen by one of the scientists running the experiment and I have to tune into that person and give them a message. They do not know they are receiving it. At the end of the test all the people present are given a sheet of paper with a list of the statements I have made and are asked to put a tick next to any information that applies to them. Strangely enough, it usually turns out that the only person who can tick all of the boxes is the person who has been chosen to receive the message.

As part of other tests, I have had my head wired up to machines that register brainwaves in order to determine my brain functions during a session of mediumship. Apparently my waves go from alpha to theta in around two minutes. I have no idea what to do with that knowledge, so I thought I would just offload it here!

I trained in my development group for approximately eight years, which is quite a long time for any apprenticeship. For the past 15 years I have been practising and demonstrating in private and public as a medium. The development of my mediumship continues as I learn from each person I meet. I have found that if I use my gift to help those who are truly grieving then more often than not there is a good result and my sitter is uplifted by the experience. If, on the other hand, I were to use my psychic abilities just to impress people or make money, I am sure the results would be less than successful.

I have also learned through experience that people who seek help from mediums should not go into the process with any preconceived ideas or expectations about what their loved one will tell them. It's best to remain open-minded and allow your-self to be given what you need, not what you think you want.

The Reason Why

More often than not I am asked, 'Why do you do mediumship?'. I often ask myself the same question, especially on a weekend when all of my friends are going out and I am heading off to give a demonstration of my work.

It was just such a day when I was working in my barber shop, feeling a bit down as a group of friends had invited me to a concert in Glasgow but I was booked to work in a Spiritualist church in Edinburgh. The entire day I moped around, asking myself, 'Why do I do mediumship?'. The time seemed to drag and the haircuts were not looking too good, as I was becoming a bit heavy-handed with the electric clippers.

Five o'clock came eventually and I prepared to close the salon. By now I was in a foul mood. All of the staff had gone and I was left to tidy the shop, still asking the spirit world the same question, when my thoughts were broken by the sound of the door opening.

Without thinking, I said loudly, 'We're closed!' Looking round, I saw a tall and well-built man in his thirties looking at me with a rather exasperated expression on his face. To cut a long story short, he wanted a shave and I eventually agreed that I would do it as I still had time to kill before going to the Spiritualist church.

As I applied the shaving cream, I had a strong impression of somebody watching me. The man was lying back in the barber's chair, face full of cream, quite relaxed by now and saying nothing. Holding my open razor to his throat I began to shave him in silence, only to feel that same sensation of somebody standing watching me. I looked up at the mirror in front of me and to my horror saw a young woman looking back at me.

I just didn't know how to react. *Who are you?* I thought.

'Judy,' she replied at once. The impression was so strong and I knew she wanted me to speak to the man beneath the razor. Normally I would never give messages to my clients, but this seemed so urgent that I had to.

'Do you know who Judy is?' I asked.

It was like an eruption – he sat bolt upright, almost joining the woman in the spirit world as I pulled the razor away from his throat just in time.

Try to imagine the scene: I am standing over a very large man whose face is half-covered with shaving cream and I'm talking to a woman in the mirror in front of him, a woman he cannot see. I really wanted to run away, but I couldn't, so I told him that I was a medium and that Judy was in the spirit world and wanted to give him a message.

It turned out that Judy was the man's wife and she had died six months earlier. As I began to describe her, he began to sob. I then asked her if she could give me some evidence that would clinch it for him. She simply said, 'Thank you for the lollipops'. I must admit I was hoping for something more earth-shattering, but her husband broke down completely at this statement. Two days earlier, he had gone to visit his wife's grave with their seven-year-old son, who had asked his father if he could take some lollipops instead of flowers to the grave.

I went on to give the man some more evidence that his wife was still alive in the spirit world and we talked for almost an hour. He told me that his wife had been so full of life and love for him and his son that he just knew she was still around them.

By the time I arrived at the Spiritualist church in Edinburgh I knew why I did mediumship. It was to prove to people that death is not the end of the human consciousness. That knowledge can heal people whose hearts are breaking.

You Cannot Die for the Life of You

Even though grieving people appear to benefit more than anyone else from mediumship, I can't help but think how many other people would benefit from the knowledge that there is life after physical death. I am sure this knowledge would shape this world in a much more contented and compassionate way. If we were to lose our fear of death, we would all live much happier lives as a result. I know that I have no fear whatsoever of death or what follows. More importantly, I have no fear of living. This is the real message I hope that my work brings to people.

I have said it many times, but you really cannot die for the life of you. After this physical life has ended, your spiritual life force goes on and on forever, changing and growing as it moves into the spirit world and beyond our human comprehension. Mediumship may just offer a little glimpse of what lies ahead, but one thing is for sure: it is a journey we will all make.

CHAPTER TWO

Life After Death

Life After Death

One of the questions most asked of those in the spirit world has to be: 'What's it like over there?'. This is natural enough – wouldn't you be curious? After all, we'll all be going there one day...

When I was beginning to learn about mediumship in my twenties, I assumed that spirit people looked like we do, only a little more glowing. This, I suppose, was due to how I would see them clairvoyantly. My instinct told me that the spirit world was a well-backlit place filled with shiny, happy people. When I imagined what it looked like, I saw white buildings and beautiful countryside with colours beyond description. It was easy to accept this, as most of the books I was reading at the time were packed with heavenly realms that fitted my own ideas of the hereafter. It wasn't until I managed to find some cassette recordings of a very rare type of phenomenon that my view changed completely.

Voices in the Dark

The mediumship of a man called Leslie Flint was different from anything I had encountered at that time. When I say 'different', I mean he didn't give messages to his sitters like mental mediums do or go into a trance and let a highly evolved spirit guide speak through him, and as for ectoplasm, there was not even a hint of the controversial misty white substance around him. It was simply that whenever he sat in a darkened room, voices would be heard in the air around him.

It first began in his childhood, back in the 1920s, when he would go to watch the silent movies at his local cinema. During the picture people around him would ask him to be quiet and stop talking, as it was putting them off the film. Leslie never understood this as he could hear the voices too, only he assumed that they were coming from someone else.

In his late teens, he tried to find out about the strange events that were occurring around him and went on to develop his gift in a Spiritualist circle. It became known as independent direct voice mediumship, so called because the voices were coming directly from the spirit people and were completely independent of the medium. All that was required of him was that he sit in a darkened room.

Now it's the dark room bit that makes you think 'fraud', but over the years that followed, Leslie Flint was tested by many scientists. Experiments would see our medium tied to a chair, gagged and holding a mouthful of coloured water, which he had to empty into a glass at the end of the test to prove that he was not a ventriloquist. I'm certain that if he had been, he could have made a good living on the variety circuit with that kind of act! A Dr Louis Young invented most of these tests and, along with members of the Society for Psychical Research, carried out further tests in infra-red light with a microphone attached to Leslie's throat. Still the voices were recorded.

During the course of many years and many investigations, no one ever accused Leslie Flint of being a trickster or fake and his gift became known all over the world. People who had lost a loved one would come from far and wide in the hope of hearing the voices of their nearest and dearest speak directly to them from beyond the grave. So many people, as it happened, that Leslie had to hold group sessions to accommodate the demand for sittings.

Each group of people would assemble in the sitting room of Leslie's London flat in anticipation. Spirit people of all descriptions would come and talk to them, not only their relatives. It was as if there was a microphone in the spirit world and the spirit people would stand in line waiting their turn to speak.

Voices would come from all corners of the room and often several would converse at once, giving detailed descriptions of their life on Earth and other pieces of personal information. All of these sessions were taped and on listening to many of them myself, I can draw only two conclusions: either fraud was being carried out by a large group of mimics who could create a wide range of voices and speak in several languages as well as know a great deal about everyone in each group or that the phenomenon, however unbelievable, was actually happening. I tend to go with the latter.

Spiritual Evolution

Some of Leslie Flint's spirit communicators became regular commentators on their progression in the spirit world and would speak freely to their families about events that had taken place since they last spoke. Common descriptions of the other side included being in great light and feeling a sense of weightlessness and contentment. There was also a sense of being drawn into a brighter light and if the same spirit had the chance to come and speak at a later session there was a noticeable sense of development in how they spoke and in their reaction to the material world.

One young man who became a frequent communicator was David Cattanach, who had died at the age of 18. He made many visits to the Leslie Flint sessions over a period of almost 10 years and spoke to his mother there. I know her personally and she is someone I would describe as very astute, someone who would not easily be fooled, especially when it came to her son, and she had no doubts that she was hearing his voice. In his earlier contacts, he spoke mainly to her, giving brief messages of comfort, but also describing his surroundings. At first these were of a fairly material nature, although filled with a sense of peace and contentment. But each time he managed to come through there was a new strength in his voice and brightness in his personality and there was even a sense of his surroundings changing.

In one of the later sessions, when one of the group asked him what it was like on the other side, David addressed the whole gathering. He started by saying that he could not conjure up the words to even begin to describe how beautiful it was there and that he felt alive in a way that he never had before. He went on to talk about how he had progressed away from the material world. He said that he was in a state of luminosity and wasn't aware of having a body any more – he still had some sort of vehicle, but it wasn't so important. In his new state he could expand his knowledge just by encountering another spirit.

Everything that they knew was shared and so each grew in awareness. His knowledge certainly seemed to be vast as he continued to talk about his understanding of the spirit world he had become a part of. He described levels of consciousness that were wonderful and open to all to discover; he described death as a great adventure that none of us should fear; he explained that all levels of life were interconnected and that our earthly level was the darkest of all, that we were limited in our understanding because of our emotions and that it was important for us to expand our consciousness beyond our limited vision of ourselves.

In the last part of his talk he spoke to his mother, telling her that no matter how he evolved, they would always be connected. For her, the most marvellous part of these encounters was hearing how her son had grown over the years.

Leslie Flint died in 1991, but most of his work was recorded and can be obtained from the foundation which was set up in his name.

Truths and Misconceptions about the Afterlife

- *White staircases, pearly gates and Saint Peter with a long white flowing beard...* No, these all went out years ago! It's no longer compulsory to wear white flowing gowns, play harps and hang around on fluffy clouds.

- *You are likely to receive wings and a halo as a reward for your good deeds or be thrown into hellfire for your bad deeds.* The truth is that this really won't happen.
- *Heaven will look like Earth with better backlighting and shiny, happy people will welcome you with hymn singing and tambourine playing.* Contrary to what I once thought, it doesn't and they won't.
- *Our father's kingdom has many mansions set out for individual religious groups.* There are no religious divisions on the other side. So, Muslims, Jews and Christians, you'll all just have to learn to get on together over there.
- *On death you become immediately enlightened.* No, you still have to progress spiritually and take responsibility for your actions in your last human existence.
- *The spirit world is all there is.* The spirit world is but the first step on your development of consciousness, so don't get too comfortable there.

Knocking on Heaven's Door

I can't actually say that I have been to the spirit world, though I have experienced altered states of consciousness and mental images of it have been imprinted on my mind by spirit communicators. Either way, even though I know the spirit world exists, I can't give a true description or pinpoint its location.

Descriptions of the hereafter have been given, however, by people who have experienced a near-death experience (NDE) or an out-of-body experience (OBE) (sound like awards, don't they?)

A typical NDE, as the name would suggest, happens when a person is close to physical death. Many people have actually been pronounced dead, only to come back with a tale of their marvellous journey.

Although the description may differ from person to person, most have a common thread running through them. First a light appears, which draws the person towards it. This is usually accompanied by a sense of travelling very fast down a tunnel. Ringing noises may also be heard. The journey into the light always seems to end at a point of stillness and contentment. Some say they see a Christ-like figure or angelic beings, others have given accounts of meeting Buddha or Mohammed, many see deceased family members. Another common feature is a voice saying that they should go back now, that it's not their time. Most people come back to full consciousness with a feeling of spiritual upliftment and no fear of dying. Often they express great joy at the indescribable sensations they felt when in this altered state of consciousness.

Many such accounts have been investigated over the years and much has been said about the cause of the experiences being a lack of oxygen in the brain, resulting in hallucinations and a feeling of euphoria. Experiments do contest this, however. Many of those who have experienced NDEs have claimed that they were conscious of conversations going on around them while they were 'dead' and some have said their spirit floated upwards and have given accurate accounts of what they saw in places they could not possibly have been physically. One test involved labels being placed above the lights in the operating theatre, where they could not be seen from the ground, and these were described accurately by several people who claimed to have experienced an NDE.

Recently I had to have a general anaesthetic before having some very intrusive exploratory tests done and I really hoped that I would have some sort of paranormal experience. As it happened, I did, but not of the NDE kind. As I began to come to,

I became aware of a lot of people standing around me in the recovery room. Some of them were writing and then I realized that I was speaking. It turned out that I had been talking during the procedure and giving messages from the spirit world to some of the theatre staff. One of the nurses told me that even though many people mumble a sort of gibberish under anaesthetic, I was actually referring to all present by their Christian names and talking about their relatives who had died. Several of the theatre staff had accompanied me to the recovery room to see if anything more would be said and then for a laugh one of the hospital porters had asked if I could give them the lottery numbers. Nobody expected an answer, but then I began to spout numbers in quick succession! Suddenly everyone was digging into their pockets for pen and paper!

Even though I had no experience of Heaven, maybe one of the hospital staff found material Heaven in the following Saturday's lottery draw...

My First Out-of-Body Experience

Thankfully I have never had a NDE, but on many occasions I have found myself in an out-of-body state.

The first time I remember this happening to me was when I was in my early twenties. I was sitting at home in my flat in Glasgow when my mind began to drift to memories of my childhood. These were happy thoughts and I began to feel more relaxed as I drifted down memory lane. Then suddenly I became aware of a sense of vibration engulfing me. At first I thought that the chair I was resting in was shaking, but as the vibrations got faster I knew that it was more to do with me. Then I felt as though I were floating up from the chair and moving towards the ceiling. I was aware of how light I had become and that I was now looking down on someone, but it took a moment to realize that that person was me!

I have no idea why, but the first thought to enter my mind was one about my workmate Sandra. No sooner had the thought registered than I was somehow in her bedroom observing her. She was sitting in a basketweave chair reading a book and looking very peaceful and calm. Then I noticed the clock on her bedroom wall and shot back into my body with a start.

The sharp return to my body startled me, yet I felt amazing. I assume that the limited thought that I had about time was what had brought me back. My body was stone cold, because even though the whole episode felt as though it had taken no more than five seconds, two hours had actually passed.

The following morning I asked Sandra what she had done the previous evening and was astounded when she told me that she had stayed at home and read a book in her room until late. I had to ask, 'Do you have a basketweave chair in your bedroom?'.

'Yes, but how do you know?'

It wasn't easy to explain.

Heaven Knows

It is very difficult for anyone to describe the feeling of being outside their own body, for there are no words to describe the sensations of lightness or stillness experienced in such a state. Similarly, it is difficult for any of us to know what life is like after death. Even with all of the spirit communications I have passed between the two worlds, it would appear that everyone who tries to describe their new surroundings gives a different account of what it looks or feels like. Is this because we all perceive things in different ways or because we gravitate to different levels of understanding in the spirit world?

One way of trying to understand what might be going on is to imagine a group of alien visitors coming to our planet and each one being sent to a different location. One might find itself in the jungles of Africa, another in the middle of New York City and another on a desert island in the Caribbean. If each of these visitors tried to describe Earth based on what they had observed in their own small corner, there would be no corroboration at all. Each would feel that their description was accurate but put together, it would not form a complete picture of this planet and all the life that exists on it. What happens in the spirit world may be something along these lines. The best we can do is speculate.

Many people have already speculated on this very subject. The 18th-century scientist Emanuel Swedenborg gave us the theory that on death the human spirit is held in a between-life waiting area where it may encounter spirit people who are familiar – family, friends and associates. His belief was that the spirit would remain in this state for a period, but would eventually be drawn to a level of like-mindedness, where it would encounter others of a similar essence, according to spiritual merits.

The idea of a between-life state also features in other religious beliefs and practices. Tibetan Buddhists believe that when we die we must go through what they call the Bardo state. This is seen as a journey taken by the consciousness at the time of physical death. At that moment it is said that a clear light will appear and if you recognize this light, you will become enlightened. Unfortunately, not many of us do so. However, there are other chances with another five coloured lights that follow. The rule of thumb is to go to the brightest one you see, as the paler, softer lights can lead you in a backwards direction. Your consciousness will move through seven stages of the Bardo during a period of 49 days. During this time, your consciousness will come face to face with many demons, which are projections of your own mind. You must try to accept them rather than run away in fear, in order to reach the brightest light that you can. Whatever state you have reached at the end of 49 days will determine your conscious state at the beginning of your new life.

Both the beliefs of Swedenborg and the practices of the Tibetan Buddhists encourage us to be more aware that we should carry out good actions in this life in order to build up a spiritual bank balance to help us in the life to come. Even if both views are wrong, they still encourage us to become better in this life and that can't be bad.

Having a belief that there is a life after death, no matter what religion or spiritual practice you follow, at least gives a sense of hope. There are of course some people who think that when we die we are dead, deceased and defunct. I think they will wake up to a great shock on the other side, a bit like having a surprise party!

The flip side of this coin was put beautifully by my good friend Professor Archie Roy, when he said, 'If I find that when I die there is no afterlife, I shall be extremely disappointed'.

The Long Kiss Goodnight

Robert Parker was a man who had no belief in God, religion or life after death. After the loss of a son early in his marriage he became totally opposed to the idea that the human spirit could continue in any way, shape or form. At the age of 68, having no known illness, he went to bed one night with his wife Barbara. Before turning to go to sleep, she kissed him on the forehead and said, 'Good night'. The following morning she was shocked to find that he was dead.

Even though her husband had been totally against the idea of visiting mediums and on many occasions had ridiculed people who spoke of such things, Barbara could not accept that he had gone out of her life forever and so she decided to look for a reputable medium to see if there was any chance that her husband was wrong about life after death.

I was sitting in a small room in a Spiritualist church in Glasgow waiting for my last appointment of the day when the door opened and in walked a nicely dressed, good-looking woman in her sixties. I began at once giving my usual spiel: 'Have you had a sitting with a medium before? This is how it works… Please don't give me any information about the person you hope to contact', etc. No sooner had I tuned into the spirit world than I heard a man's voice saying, 'I was wrong, I was wrong, please tell Barbara I was wrong'.

Once he got started, there was no stopping him! He told me that his name was Bobby, which was how his wife had always referred to him, and that he was with Raymond, who was the son they had lost early in their marriage. The sitting was packed with information about his life and with small details which his wife understood and which were relevant to their life together.

Near the end of the sitting the mood changed somewhat, as Bobby began to relate how he had found himself in the spirit world. He recalled that he had gone to bed in his home and had woken up after a beautiful sleep in a room that was filled with light. To his surprise, there was a nurse there holding his long-lost baby son Raymond. He then talked of meeting his parents and other family members and friends who were dead – only they weren't! His wife was able to place all of the people he claimed he had met. He gave no great description of his surroundings, but spoke of a state of grace and comfort that he said he could not explain in words.

The message ended with Bobby reminiscing, 'The last thing that you said to me was "Good night" and I remember that you turned and kissed me on the head'. He said this was the first thing he remembered when he woke.

Bobby may have been dead against the idea of an afterlife, but he is a good example of what mediums have said for years: that you cannot die for the life of you!

God's Waiting Room

For most of my adult life I have tried to understand what it feels like to actually die (I know, it's sad, isn't it?). During that time I have seen, heard, felt and held conversations with spirit people, at times under the strictest of scientific conditions. I have also experienced leaving my body, being engulfed by white light and having what I can best describe as spiritual experiences. Yet no matter what I have felt or witnessed, I still find it very difficult to comprehend what it is like in the spirit world. No matter how we try to envisage it, all we can do is compare it to our earthly lives. Maybe that's why so many of the descriptions of the afterlife still seem to be based on a materialistic world and involve loving reunions with radiant departed relatives.

As a medium I find it hard to believe that when we die we hang around God's waiting room for all of our relatives and friends to arrive, with no other purpose than to act as a welcoming committee. I'm sure there's more to the next life than that. Certainly, though, it would seem that there is some kind of reunion with our loved ones. So many nurses and carers have witnessed a dying person reach out and speak to an unseen person who they claim has come to collect them and take them into the other side. Similarly, many of those who have experienced an NDE have mentioned spirit relatives waiting to greet them, as did many of the communicators over the years at the Leslie Flint sessions. There may also be a connection to other individuals who have shared a part of our lives and have formed a spiritual bond with us.

It has occurred to me that the welcoming committee is there because becoming a spirit in a realm of bright light may be too much for the conscious mind to take in. Is the afterlife so bright that we have to wear shades? We may have to acclimatize and limit our view of the true spiritual experience with what our mind can accept at that moment. So the afterlife may appear to be a brilliant version of this life until our consciousness can adjust and gravitate to its own level of awareness. Even in this human form we have the ability to create different views of reality – so often we choose to see what we want to see and not what is real. Does the same apply after death? Yet the more we grow in spirit and adapt to our new reality, the less attached we will become to human ways and conditions and the clearer our vision will become.

From our current standpoint, dying is the most major event we will ever have to face. What can make us more accepting of death? Is it the hope that stems from the knowledge that we live again? Or could it be that we have to reach a point of understanding that we are spirits already and that physical death is no more than a change of environment?

After thinking long and hard about what life will be like when we die, I'm convinced that so much is dependent on our life now and on our state of mind at the moment of death. To prepare yourself for that inevitable journey you must begin to take responsibility for all that you are in this life, to look at your life with clarity and assess it with truth. It seems that our delusions about what life holds for us in the hereafter arise from our delusions about who we are in the here and now. If we can accept that we are already spirit beings living in a spirit realm, we can accept that death is not so much a journey to a different world but to a different state of mind.

CHAPTER THREE

Heaven and Hell

Heaven and Hell

Some of the most common questions I am asked about the afterlife concern Heaven and Hell. Many people fear that loved ones who have led less than perfect lives are held in some 'dark Hell realm'.

On one occasion back in 1996 I was giving a private sitting in London to a middle-aged woman. She was well dressed and looked physically strong and healthy, but her sadness was apparent to me the moment that I took her hand. Then I could hear the voice of a young man in the spirit world telling me that this was his mother. I sensed the presence of a very tall slim man in his early twenties, someone who felt awkward and uneasy and withdrawn. As always, I asked for the name of the communicator, but this time nothing came back at me.

'How did you die?' I asked the young man.

'I don't know,' he replied at once.

Whenever I am communicating with someone who finds it difficult to give information I ask the spirit world if there is anyone else around who can help them. I had no sooner sent out this thought than an older lady came through much more strongly and said her name was Dorothy.

I told my sitter that Dorothy was helping the young man to communicate. She looked straight at me and said, 'Is she?'. It turned out that Dorothy was her mother-in-law.

Dorothy passed on a great deal of relevant information about her life and family, including her grandson, whose name was Mike. She explained that he had been suffering from AIDS and knew that he was going to die very soon. One night he had simply decided to take some tablets from the bathroom and end it all rather than involve everyone around him in prolonged emotional suffering. His family had already died a social death with other family members, neighbours and so-called friends.

Then Mike himself began to communicate. He told his mother that he was free of his suffering now and that he wanted to stop her from hurting too. He knew that she believed he was in some sort of limbo or purgatory because of what he had done. Such was her torment that she had consulted a medium even though it was against her religious beliefs.

In fact, the only Hell that was experienced in this instance was the Hell that Mike's mother had put herself through because of her beliefs and conditioning. Once she was free of this self-imposed prison a great burden was lifted from her and she found the freedom to communicate with her son in the spirit world, where he seemed to be happy and at peace.

'Free at Last'

On another occasion, during a public demonstration I was giving in Spain in 1996, a spirit woman communicated with her sister in the audience. She described how she had never felt loved or appreciated in her marriage and how her life had become Hell. In 10 years of married life she had never produced a child and as a result had felt that her husband had stopped loving her. He was cheating and lying and finally she had simply ended her life by hanging herself. She described her last feelings on Earth as those of a baby lying in a darkened room, alone and screaming for help, with no one around to lift her or care for her or take away her pain.

It had been her sister who had found her body and now the spirit woman felt she had to communicate with her to tell her how sorry she was that she had found her in such a terrible state. She wanted her to try to move on and not to dwell on the horrible scene she had encountered. As evidence of her survival, she gave names, dates and addresses relating to her former life, as well as mentioning many events she had shared with her sister. She explained that her life on the other side was very happy and that she was surrounded by loving people who were helping her to progress.

At the end of the demonstration I made a point of speaking to the sister in private. She told me that she had been unable to move on with her own life because of the thought of her sister suffering in some inferno realm as the result of her suicide. She had even offered her own suffering to try to release her. She told me of her joy at hearing that her sister was not in purgatory after all, but was being helped to move forward. Now she too was prepared to go on with her life and accept happiness again.

I can only conclude from this account that if there truly is such a state of suffering as purgatory, then it exists only in this human world. It is experienced when we are lacking in love, either for ourselves or from those close to us. I can think of no greater emptiness in life than this.

Truths and Misconceptions about Heaven and Hell

- *Hell is a physical place located beneath the ground on this planet.* Surely the Earth's surface would have collapsed by now with the number of people being held there, and it would be getting worse by the second.

- *If you go to Hell you will roast in everlasting torment.* Again, I don't think so. Fire can only harm the physical body; our spirit is indestructible and eternal. This is a very human way of looking at suffering in the afterlife.

- *The Devil is a big guy with horns on his head, carrying a large trident and wearing a red outfit.* This wouldn't work, would it? These days there are characters in children's computer games that look more frightening than that!

- *Heaven is a place where you can indulge in endless sensory pleasures.* No, I'm sorry to disappoint the woman in London who was hoping to meet her many lovers again, but in Heaven there is no need for that type of pleasure!

- *Hell has many levels, like different units of a prison where the really bad dudes are in the high-security wings and the young offenders are in some sort of open-air division.* No, the real Hell is not subdivided like this. It is a state experienced by people who are locked in personal torment.

- *If you sin in this life you will go straight to Hell and your soul will be trapped there forever.* Living with the emotional pain we feel in this life when we are aware that we have done wrong has to be punishment enough. If we grow from such an experience, no afterlife judgement is needed.

The Sisters Grim

If we look at both Heaven and Hell as states of mind, then Hell can be perceived as the product of our own way of thinking and our own emotions. Unfortunately we may come to believe that this is our punishment or just desserts rather than our choice.

An experience that I had when sitting for two sisters in Germany some years ago showed me how some people find it easier to condemn themselves to their own little world of hate than to try to find love.

Ida and Irma's sitting began with their father trying to communicate from the other side. He told me that he had been over there for 30 years, but the women just looked at each other, shrugged their shoulders, looked back at me and said together, in heavily accented English, 'Why would our father want to speak to us? We hate him!'.

I felt rather puzzled, but continued, 'He gives me the name of Abe and says that he would like to help you.'

'Why would he help us now, after so long, when we can't stand him? What does he really want and is there anybody else we can speak to?'

'Hold on,' I said. Then, 'Nora Schuster is here. Do you know her?'

At once they called out, 'We hate her, why is she here? This is our aunt who brought us up when we were children.'

I ignored this outburst and proceeded to pass Nora's message to the sisters, which was that they should look back over their lives and try to understand some of what their family went through for them, then make contact with their brother Ben and reunite the family.

At this both women gave a little shrug and Ida broke into my speech. 'Stop this and let me explain something to you.' She told me that their Aunt Nora had raised them while their father had given all of his time to his business. She claimed that her aunt had paid more attention to her own children than to them and that their older brother had 'abandoned' them by going to live in America. What they really wanted to know was whether they would ever be happy in their lives as they had been sad for so many years.

When I heard this last statement I almost burst out laughing, but I managed to keep my composure and tried to explain to them that they were creating sadness for themselves and that the hate they felt was harming no one but themselves. I asked if they would like to change their lives and find some form of happiness. After a quick glance at each other, they agreed. Then I told them to call their brother and see if they could visit him in the States.

'But we hate him...' Irma began.

I had to interrupt. 'Stop! Please listen to my advice and think about what I have asked you to do.'

The sitting ended with both women looking more miserable than when they had first entered the room and I felt I had not done a very good job. But the following morning as I was walking through the hotel lobby I heard a voice calling, 'Wait, wait!'. It was the sisters, both smiling and running towards me with short little steps. Both grabbed my arm at once and began to tell me of their revelation.

It turned out that after much deliberation they had called their brother in New York, only to find that he was delighted to hear from them, as one of his sons was getting married and his family really wanted to invite their long-lost aunts over for the wedding and to spend time with them. Their brother thought that they would not come because they hated him! But to his amazement they told him that they would love to attend the wedding and become reacquainted with him and his family. After all, as Ida said, 'How could we hate our own family?'.

A Pain in the Neck

Of course, taking responsibility for our own behaviour is not always straightforward. It is always easier to lay the blame on someone else.

Before I demonstrated as a medium, I used to practise spiritual healing in our little Spiritualist church in Glasgow. It was during this time that I first became aware of how some people seemed to be content in their misery. It was excellent training for someone like me who was trying to bring hope to the hopeless!

I sometimes wondered if some of my best healing in those days wasn't done in the hairdressing salon where I worked. As women who make appointments regularly know, hairdressing is the highest form of counselling – not only can you offload all your troubles, but you come out looking a million dollars!

One of the people I used to see each week at the healing clinic was a lady called Georgia. She was in her mid-fifties and very dowdy. She lived with her husband and son, both named Tom. Young Tom was in his early thirties. Georgia needed healing for the mysterious pain she was suffering at the base of her neck. She had had every X-ray and examination on offer, but no doctor had ever been able to offer a diagnosis.

After each healing session was over I would spend a short time talking to Georgia about her healing and asking after her family. She always seemed down whenever she mentioned both husband and son, saying things like 'They have ruined my life' or 'It is because of them that I am in such pain'. I felt so sorry for her, as she always seemed so unhappy.

After some months of healing sessions it was becoming clear to me that my talks with Georgia were becoming longer and I felt as if I was becoming part of her life. I knew almost everything about the two men in her life — how they didn't include her in anything they did and how she felt separate from them. She told me that she had even thought of ending her life, but she thought that would make them happy!

Now if Georgia had been a client in my hairdressing salon, I would have advised her to tint her hair blonde, change her wardrobe and demand attention, but she wasn't, so I just listened.

It became more and more apparent that she would not make any effort to be happy. In fact, her feelings towards her family were turning into a silent hatred. Along with this, she was suffering more physical pain and even starting to find her mobility restricted.

One day I really prayed hard during the healing session that Georgia would be happy and that her pains would decrease. Then I suddenly heard myself speaking out loud, telling her that she would have to learn to make her own happiness and include herself in the lives of her husband and son. Once I had begun, there was no stopping. By the end of the session Georgia was in tears. She told me that she knew that she was causing her own misery and creating Hell in her home. Her husband did not know what to do with her and her son was afraid of her frequent rages. She had been pushing both men away from her and she knew it. No matter how many times she tried to blame them, inside she could feel that it was her own doing.

As soon as Georgia admitted that she was responsible for her problems, she felt a weight lift from her shoulders. Over the weeks that followed she became stronger and more positive. For our last session she turned up with tastefully tinted hair, wearing a smart skirt and blouse and looking so happy and alive. She thanked me for all the healing and told me that she and Tom senior were going off on holiday. Then she remarked, 'I feel as though I'm in Heaven!'.

To witness such a change of heart is wonderful. So many people never seem to progress emotionally or mentally in life, yet no state of mind is permanent unless we choose to make it so. By examining our thinking and exercising some control over our emotions, we can all gain enough awareness to break free of our negative patterns. We all encounter difficult experiences in our lives, but we can learn to grow from them.

'Walking a Step Behind'

The shock of bereavement is one difficult experience which can affect our state of mind a great deal, even take us into a different state of consciousness which may be our own personal form of Hell. One woman who had recently lost her young son in a terrible motor accident described this to me very vividly.

'I feel as if I'm walking a step behind my body,' she began, 'and my thinking is out of sync with the places and people I encounter. Even when people speak to me I become aware of what they are thinking more than what they are saying, as if I have become stuck in a world of thought and am unable to become a part of real life again.'

This reminded me of how a medium feels when they experience an altered state of consciousness in order to make a stronger link with the spirit world. When in this state they will experience a feeling of separateness from their body and a sense of being out of reality. Their sensitivity heightens in such a way that they become more in tune with a more subtle atmosphere.

The grieving woman even talked about a kind of numbness, like being in limbo, which she felt was safe because while in this state she neither had to look back nor forward. Her limbo had become a haven away from 'normality'. Even in this mental void, however, something deep down was nagging away at her to get back into life.

The sitting had a big effect on her. 'It was like electricity hitting me, bringing me back to life.' This was the spirit of her son affecting her consciousness and jump-starting it back into human reality. Again, this type of electrical surge is felt by trance mediums when they flit from one state of consciousness to another. The upshot of the experience was that the woman no longer felt disconnected and alone in her grief, but was prepared to re-enter normal reality. Tough as that would be, she was no longer in a state of limbo.

Judgement Day

So many views of the afterlife are based on the idea of a judgement, after which the good people go to Heaven and the bad people go to Hell. But who is all good in their life or all bad? How good do we have to be to get through the pearly gates and what is bad enough for the eternal toasting? If decent young men get sent off to war and are asked to kill decent young men in the name of democracy, is this worthy of an eternal stay in the fiery Hell or are they granted a get-out-of-jail-free card on some moral technicality? And who decides?

While attending a book signing by a well-known psychic in Glasgow, I asked him if he had ever seen or sensed someone from the spirit world. He told the packed bookshop that he hoped that he never would, as when he was a young man doing national service for his country he had killed someone on the opposing side. He explained that it was a case of kill or be killed, but that memory had haunted him ever since and he wondered if he would have to face the young soldier when he died. Isn't it Hell to try and live with such a heavy burden? And is that enough or should this man be punished further after death? I believe that the remorse he feels in this life and what he has learned from the situation will balance out his karmic debt.

One of the Spiritualist religion's principles, which I know is echoed in other spiritual practices, is that we should take personal responsibility for our own actions. This is how we measure our growth in this life. When I am asked where 'bad' people will go in the next life I try to explain that people are not really bad when they come into this world, but they may carry out bad actions – and that is our human side. We all make mistakes. To become aware of them and admit to them is a way of lightening our load and moving forward. To repeat the same things time after time is foolish and can be seen as not learning our lessons.

As I understand it, in this lifetime we will experience both Heaven and Hell, love and hate. We will all feel the full spectrum of emotions, we will all move through our own Heavens and Hells, but learning to accept and grow from them is the natural journey our consciousness wants to make.

We are all capable of creating either Heaven or Hell. Both belong in this human existence and both are simply experiences that we can learn from.

CHAPTER FOUR

Ghosts and Spirits

Ghosts and Spirits

People have always been fascinated by ghosts, spirits and things that go bump in the night. Even children love the chill and suspense of a good ghost story. My own sons used to ask me to tell them such tales when they were younger, only now I think they would be more reluctant in case they got the real thing!

The idea of anyone, or thing for that matter, returning from beyond the grave is usually seen as creepy and horrible. It is as if we have been programmed to think that anything coming back from death would be evil and might even want to steal our souls. Then we frighten ourselves even more with our own imaginings. Any child in a darkened bedroom can turn a white shirt on a doorknob into all sorts of ghosts and ghouls.

If only people understood the real phenomena, they could say to their children that where ghosts and spirits are concerned, there really is nothing to be afraid of and that the fear we feel comes from ourselves.

This was the case with my first official haunting.

My First Haunted House

Not long after I had begun to work as a medium, my teacher Mrs Primrose took me along to a house where the family were being disturbed by what they said was the ghost of an elderly man. His appearances were becoming more frequent and were being experienced by more and more people.

I had never been to an official haunting before and I remember asking Mrs P. what we could expect to happen during our encounter with the elderly phantom. She explained to me that we would ask each person to give an account of what they had experienced and try to put together a picture of the ghost and to find out if there was any particular reason from within the family that caused him to appear. Then we would, if need be, tune into the spirit world and find out if there was any spiritual activity that needed to be addressed or if what was happening was 'just a ghost' or even down to the imagination of the people concerned.

We arrived at the house and to my surprise it was very modern. I suppose I thought it would be an old house standing in its own grounds. Mr and Mrs Thompson and their teenage son and daughter were standing in the small front hall, together with their neighbour, who had also seen the alleged ghost.

Mrs P. questioned each person in turn while I listened. All of the accounts were practically identical: around nine o'clock at night an elderly man was seen wearing dark trousers and a white shirt with old-fashioned braces hanging at the side of his trousers. Everyone agreed that he would appear for a few seconds and then vanish into thin air.

Mrs P. had a strong sense that there wasn't a spirit trying to communicate or get noticed for any reason, but said she would tune in and see if she could sense any psychic history in the area of the sightings. I watched as she closed her eyes for a moment and then spoke about a farm and a James Patterson who had died alone and very sad. She also gave other details about Mr Patterson's life, which I noted for further investigation.

Then Mrs P. spoke to all the people together and told them that they had nothing to worry about as what they were seeing was '*only a ghost*'. I remember thinking, Only a ghost! Mrs P. explained that this was just a memory of someone's life trapped in time and that it might be seen again, but it could not interact with this world as it was only a visual phenomenon and not a spirit, angry or otherwise.

The Thompson family and their neighbour seemed to be quite relieved by this explanation and thanked us both for coming. Mr Thompson said he would try to find out some of the history of the place and see if he could trace Mr Patterson and the farm.

It must have been just two weeks later that Mr and Mrs Thompson came along to our Spiritualist church to see Mrs P. They explained that they had looked into the history of the land on which their house was built and been astonished to find that according to the old plans they came across, the very spot where their ghost appeared was previously part of an old farmhouse. It was even more surprising for them to learn that the last owners of the farm, some 20 years earlier, were a Mr and Mrs J. Patterson. Since Mrs P. and I had visited the house there had been no more sightings of the ghost.

Ghostly activity such as this can be triggered by a person who is giving off strong emotional vibes and of course, when others learn about it, their fear level goes up and can help to set it off again. Often when the fear factor is removed, the phenomenon ceases, as in this case.

Such phantom-like visions seem to be programmed to play out past actions that have taken place at that spot. They are a memory trapped in time that can be replayed, given the right conditions, just like a videotape that can be watched when the play button is pressed.

You have to wonder what could cause such a thing to happen, but most people who have seen ghosts have reported that they appear to be in a highly emotional state. If this is so, then all that is being witnessed is the stain or memory of an emotional episode in a person's life that has left its impression on a time and place.

This, I feel, accounts for two things that often feature in sightings of ghosts. The first is the appearance of phantoms without heads or screaming as if in pain or appearing to be very sombre and depressed. The second is that strong emotions such as fear, depression or rage are often felt by the people witnessing these apparitions. Is this because it is not only the audiovisual impressions that have been trapped but also the emotional anguish? If a person can remember their own emotional state at the time of their encounter with a ghost, it can make it easier to understand the emotional telepathy which flicked the 'ghost switch' and caused the videotape to be played again.

Not all reports of apparitions turn out to be of the ghostly kind, however. On some occasions the visions speak to people or give messages. These aren't ghosts, but spirits who have returned for some reason.

The Blue Ring

One Sunday in December 1994, I took my sons for a drive to a small town called Callander, about an hour from Glasgow. While I was there I found myself looking in an old junk shop. My son Steven was drawn to a ring made of lapis lazuli in one of the old glass cases and asked me if I would buy it. I wondered why he wanted such a thing, but asked the shopkeeper if I could take it from the case for him to try. Then Steven said it was not for him and that I should have it. I must admit that when I picked up the ring I really did like it and decided that if it fitted then I would buy it. I tried it on, but it didn't fit any of my fingers, much to Steven's disappointment. The shopkeeper told me that it was the only one she had and that she couldn't even remember where she had got it from. When we left the little shop I told my son that I would look for another ring like it and he simply said, 'You will get one soon, Dad'.

The following evening my old teacher Mrs Primrose was in her little flat preparing Christmas gifts for her family and friends. She left them all neatly piled on her sideboard, each with a little tag bearing the name of the recipient, but for me she left just a tag with my name and works telephone number on top of her telephone. Then she sat in her chair and gracefully passed into the spirit world. The following morning she was found by her home help, who called me at work to tell me as she had found my name and number where Mrs P. had left it. I was shocked when I was told of the news, but when I learned that Mrs P. had a broad smile across her face, I knew that she would be fine on the other side.

That evening Mrs P.'s daughter, May, told me that her mother had left a gift for everyone she knew but me. She had found this rather strange, as she was certain that her mother would have wanted me to have something, but I assured her that she had given me enough in life to remember her by.

The following day I had a phone call from my friend Dronma, who is a psychic artist. She asked me if Mrs Primrose had died, as she had appeared in her bedroom in spirit form in the early hours of the morning, smiling broadly, and had spoken to her calmly, asking her if she could go to Callander and buy a blue ring for me from the old junk shop there.

I was quite amazed by what Dronma had said. I explained to her about the ring I had seen in Callander the day before Mrs P.'s passing, but told her it did not fit me and that she needn't bother going to fetch it, as I would look for another. I was too late, though, as Dronma had already driven over early that morning, as Mrs P. had insisted the ring was to be my Christmas gift from her.

As bizarre as all of this seems, I can assure you that every bit of it is true, yet the strangest part of this story happened when I actually received the ring. I thought I would wear it around my neck on a chain, as it did not fit my fingers and there is no way I could have a ring made of stone adjusted, but when it was handed to me, my first reaction was to try it on my middle finger, and though previously it had been too big, now it fitted as if made specially for that finger.

When Mrs P. died I had thought that I would somehow hear from her again, but I didn't think it would be so soon, and how clever she was to appear to Dronma, who lives in a village next to Callander.

Spirit people tend to like to tie up their unfinished business and, if they can, help people they have left behind. They usually don't appear just for the sake of it and very often they will appear to someone other than close family or friends because otherwise their loved ones might believe that they had just created the visit out of their own emotional need.

Return to the Shopkeeper

Tricia Robertson is the vice president of the Scottish Society for Psychical Research (SSPR) and secretary of PRISM

(Psychical Research Involving Selected Mediums). She is also the co-author of two scientific papers on psychical research. She has investigated many different cases of psychic phenomena, many of which are listed in her forthcoming book, *The Uninvited*. The account that follows is from Tricia's book and deals with what I would call 'spirit return'.

A shopkeeper, Muhammad Khan, known to me for many years, was recently redecorating a room in his home and was painting quite happily at the highest point of a bedroom ceiling when suddenly there he was, four feet away from his face: a customer who used to come into his shop. He was at the same height from the floor, just under ceiling level, and about four feet away horizontally. Khan noted that he was only visible from the waist upwards, was wearing an olive green shirt and a tweed jacket and that his face was totally lifelike.

This vision then pointed at him and said, in a very animated manner, 'Tell them not to do it – everything will be all right'. In a state of shock, Khan simply stared at him. He repeated his message adamantly and then disappeared just as quickly as he had appeared.

Shaking with the shock and disbelief, Khan came down the ladder very slowly, as he was in grave danger of falling off it, and even after several cups of tea he was unable to do any more work that evening. He thought back and realized that this man had died over six years ago.

The next day he attended to his shop as usual and was happy to forget the happenings of the previous evening. However, the following day the widow of the 'apparition' came into the shop and this posed a serious problem – should he tell her about his experience or not? He eventually plucked up the courage. Her reaction was to throw her arms around him and thank him, saying that she had already been given similar information by someone else and this confirmed it. Khan was bewildered, as he did not have a clue as to what it was all about.

About two weeks later this lady offered an explanation. It transpired that her son had been wrongly accused of a crime and the family had thought of taking him to Ireland to hide, which would obviously have meant that he could not appear at court. Had they done so, the young man would have been in trouble for the rest of his life, but when he did finally appear in court, contrary to all their expectations, the case was dismissed.

Khan had never experienced anything like this before and has not done so since and he is known to me as a trustworthy person. In case the sceptic thinks that he rushed to tell me of this tale, he did not. It was only during a chance conversation with him that these details emerged and he only told it to me in the knowledge that I would not think that he had gone completely crazy.

I never did ask if the redecoration of the room was ever completed!

In this case the spirit was returning to give advice that would help his family in a time of great need. Why he chose this particular man and in this particular situation, who can say? Maybe his wife would have put it down to wishful thinking if she had experienced it herself. What I am certain of is that this was not a ghost, but a spirit still conscious and concerned about the welfare of his family. I have often found that spirits are drawn to us in times of need in our lives. It's not that they are watching us every minute of the day, but it is when we need them most that they seem to be closest to us.

Apparitions like this may be startling, but should not be seen as evil or malevolent. Cases of 'spirit return' normally bring comfort and do not leave any sense of fear. If the information the spirits give is helpful, then the experience should be looked on as a completely positive one.

The Night Shift

There are many reasons why spirits return. More often than not, all they wish to do is comfort a loved one or try to guide them. The fear we feel is not because the spirit has come to frighten us, but more to do with the unexpected nature of the experience. Even as a tried and tested medium who is used to encountering spirit people, I still get a start if I wake in the early hours and find someone standing beside my bed just looking into my face. I would often jump with fright when I woke in the early hours to find my son Steven, aged about 3 years old, standing beside my bed staring into my face. Anyone whose child has done this will know what I mean! That fear is similar to suddenly seeing a spirit, but once you become accustomed to what is happening the fear immediately goes.

A friend of mine once asked me if I would come to her house as she kept feeling that there was someone standing in her bedroom in the early hours and this was disturbing her sleep and leaving her feeling exhausted in the morning.

When I went into her bedroom I immediately felt the presence of a spirit lady standing by the dressing table, which stood opposite the bed. Within seconds she was communicating with me, so I knew at once that this was not a ghost. She told me she was my friend's aunt and she had only come to be close to her as she had just ended a relationship with her boyfriend and would cry herself to sleep at night. She would get close to her niece, but then she would wake and become frightened. The fear of being haunted would fill her mind and keep her awake until it was daylight.

When my friend found out it was her loving aunt who was coming to watch over her, she lost all her fear. She confessed that she had thought it was the ghost of a murderer who was trying to kill her! She also told me that her aunt had worked as a nurse and preferred to work night shift, so it was a habit of hers, I suppose, to look in on people during the night.

Truths and Misconceptions about Ghosts and Spirits

- *Ghosts look like people covered with a white sheet with holes cut out for the eyes and mouth.* I think that image belongs to a different kind of organization! And a ghost will never say 'Boo!' to frighten you.

- *Ghosts come to give messages from the hereafter.* In fact, ghosts don't really have a function. They are no more than memories trapped in time and place.

- *Ghosts walk through walls.* If it seems as though they do, it's only because that wall did not exist in their time frame.

- *Ghosts set out to frighten people.* People usually become afraid because of the sudden ghostly activity, that's all.

- *An exorcism or high religious ritual will rid you of a ghost.* No, the only way to stop it is to find out what emotion in you set it off and to change the way you feel.

- *Spirits who have returned from beyond the grave look like rotting corpses or zombies.* Sometimes spirits are transparent, but usually they just look like normal people – and they certainly wouldn't be seen dead at a haunted house!

The Hooded Monks

A classic ghost sighting that came to my attention recently is one that has been taking place in a residential care facility for adults with learning difficulties in the southwest of Scotland. Staff on night duty have claimed to hear footsteps when there is no one around and voices speaking in whispers in one of the corridors, and at all times of the day staff members have reported a shadowy figure on a wall, which always just appears, passes by and then disappears.

The most common complaint is of a hooded monk. In fact it turns out that there are several different descriptions of this monk. Some say his habit is one colour while others say it is another; the hood may differ or even size of the figure himself.

One of the best witnesses interviewed by the psychic researchers investigating the case was one of the day attendants. She claimed to have entered her office to find a tall thin bearded man wearing a brown monk's habit and looking very sad standing right in front of her. He went about his business as if she was not there or he was unaware of her. She was startled and picked up a feeling of sadness from him.

This case is still being investigated, but all of what has gone on in this very ordinary modern building is typical of ghostly activities. It has become more interesting of late, as the investigators have recently discovered that the care home was built on the site of an orchard that belonged to an adjoining church, which for a time was used by many different orders of monks who visited this part of Scotland from many parts of the world. This may explain the varied descriptions of the habits and hoods.

Again, as is common with this type of haunting, the characters and events belong in another time and even though they might encroach on this one, there is no interaction between the two.

Last Orders

I was recently invited to an old pub just outside Glasgow where the staff had been complaining about ghosts and other spooky happenings. It just so happened that I was taking part in some filming for a television programme at the time and everyone involved agreed to allow the ghostbusting, for want of a better term, to be filmed.

The pub was a typical village public house with small bar area leading through to a larger lounge area. Nothing looked out of the ordinary until the film crew, the psychic investigators and I were led up an old stair into an abandoned room above the pub. As usual when working with psychic researchers, I was not allowed to be given any information about the nature of the haunting, but they had taken statements from all of the people who had experienced the paranormal events.

The room was dark and dusty and had not been in use for many years by the look of it, but as a medium I had to put the physical surroundings out of my mind and tune into the finer energies.

I was immediately drawn to the far wall of the room where there was a hole where a fireplace once was, but my intuition told me that there were no spirits of the past lingering around. I stopped there and asked in my mind if there were any spirits wishing to communicate. I felt nothing, so I tuned in psychically and tried to read some of the emotional history of the place. All the while the cameras were rolling and the researchers were listening to see if I could corroborate any of the stories given by the bar staff.

In my mind's eye I could see an elderly man standing against the fireplace and then sitting down on a bench beside it as he spoke to someone very young. I knew that the original fireplace was still in the pub somewhere, that it had been taken from this room and moved to another. Then I heard loud footsteps walking across the floor, but still I felt no spirit presence. Psychically I picked up the names 'Jimmy Reid' and 'Lizzie Mac'. It was at this point that the manager spoke and said that these were people in his family. Jimmy used to own the building in which we stood. He had been dead for many years. Lizzie, the aunt of the young manager, was still alive.

Now this is where it all got strange, but became apparent to me why I was there. I spoke to the manager and said that I sensed nothing untoward or threatening about the place, but that there was someone on the other side who wished to make contact with the woman I had mentioned.

As far as the haunting of the building went, several of the bar staff had heard footsteps walking in the room above them when they were alone in the pub and one young boy had said that an elderly man had come and sat beside the fireplace in the downstairs bar and he could hear him speaking as though rambling in a past conversation. It turned out that that very fireplace had come from the room upstairs where I had sensed this. All of these events relating to the old building were just stored in the atmosphere of the old place, but I had sensed separately that the previous owner, Lizzie, had someone in the spirit world who wished to communicate with her and had taken the opportunity to make this known to me.

The film crew and all of the other people involved sat chatting in the bar after we had finished filming and I was approached by the manager, who said that Lizzie was his aunt and would it be possible for me to see her at some point in the future.

Two weeks later, I gave a private sitting to Lizzie Mac. Her husband in the spirit world had spent most of his life running the 'haunted pub' with his wife and had passed away just two years earlier. He told me he knew how much she missed him and that he had had to get back to convince her that he was still around.

As Lizzie said herself, 'I might have known he would still be hanging around that bar.'

Things That Go Bump in the Night

Things that go bump in the night always send a shiver down our spine, but often it is our lack of understanding that makes us afraid rather than the paranormal events themselves. On all of the occasions when I have helped to investigate cases of hauntings, ghosts and so-called earthbound spirits, I have never come up against anything which left me scared. I admit that there have been moments when I have been startled by a sudden noise or vision or when, say, an object has moved or floated in front of me, defying the laws of physics. But because I understand what is going on, I still manage to accept the situation and try to tune into the unseen energies to discover what is behind it all.

More often than not I feel quite relieved when I am asked to go to a place where people are frightened of a particular phenomenon and can help them to understand it or remove it, as is the case with more powerful disturbances from the unseen forces. There are times when I have felt like a psychic Rentokill being asked to get rid of pesky psychic disturbances. But my motto has become 'The more I experience, the less I fear'.

Like the child who imagines all sorts of monsters in a darkened bedroom at night, we must learn that to get rid of the monsters we only have to put on the light – in this case, the light of understanding.

CHAPTER FIVE

Poltergeists and Hauntings

Poltergeists and Hauntings

Poltergeist activities and hauntings are very different from apparitions of ghosts and spirits. It is amazing to witness furniture or ornaments and other objects moving independently around a room as if being pushed or lifted by an invisible force. Yet there is always an explanation if you look for it.

Maxwell Park

I was just 12 years old when I first heard the term 'poltergeist'. At that time all the newspapers in Scotland were reporting the paranormal goings on in a house in the area I was brought up in. One of the boys involved in this case went to my school and, kids being what they are, most of us poked fun at him about the ghostly carry on. In adulthood I became acquainted with one of the psychical researchers who had investigated the case, Professor Archie Roy of Glasgow University, who is now not only a good friend of mine but also one of the leading authorities on psychical research.

Professor Roy's account of the case can be found in his book *A Sense of Something Strange*. It involves three families, whose names have been changed for obvious reasons: the Uppinghams and the Downies, who lived in council flats in the Maxwell Park area of Glasgow, and the Schwarz family, who lived about a quarter of a mile away. Mrs Schwarz was the sister of Mrs Uppingham.

Mr and Mrs Uppingham were aged between 40 and 45 and lived on the first floor flat of the house in Maxwell Park with their sons Ian, aged 14, who was in the year above me at school, and David, 11, as well as Mrs Uppingham's mother, who was 70. In the flat beneath them lived the Downie family. Mr and Mrs Downie were both aged between 65 and 70 and their son Frank was about 30.

The first phase of poltergeist phenomena began in November 1974. The Uppinghams started hearing banging sounds echoing around their house, which they felt sure were coming from the flat downstairs. Finally Mr Uppingham could stand it no longer, so he called the police. When the police arrived they asked the Downie family about the disturbance, but Mr Downie claimed the noise was coming from the flat above and not from his home. The police gave him a warning and left. Within a short space of time Mr Uppingham called the police back to the house, as the noise had got louder. This time the police took the Downie family to the station for questioning, but the noises continued. For the first time Mr Uppingham realized that something more was involved in this disturbance.

In the days that followed all sorts of people became involved – joiners, plumbers, electricians and other building specialists as well as people from the town council – all trying to find a logical explanation to the problem, but nothing was found and the disturbances continued. Only now a new phase had started – objects were being lifted by an unseen force and thrown around the rooms in the upstairs house. So disturbing was it that the Uppingham family fled to their relations, the Schwarz family. However, as Professor Roy says, 'Of course in true poltergeist fashion, it, whatever it was, moved with them and set up home in the Schwarz house.'

It was at this point that the Faculty of Divinity from the University of Glasgow was called in to conduct a service at Maxwell Park, assisted by the Rev. Max Magee. The service was successful in ending the phenomena there. At the Schwarz house, however, the strange occurrences were being witnessed by more and more people, some of whom at first believed them to be some form of trickery but eventually became convinced they were paranormal. A local priest was called in to perform an exorcism there and after that all appeared to be calm. Relieved, the Uppinghams moved back to Maxwell Park.

Back at Maxwell Park, however, the disturbances started all over again. Objects were thrown, the banging became even louder and tables were levitating. The Rev. Max Magee and Professor Roy witnessed many of these phenomena and recorded them on audiotape. Then a third phase began, which concerned everyone, as the two boys, Ian and David Uppingham, started experiencing spontaneous contortions of their bodies.

Spiritualist mediums were now invited to hold séances to rid the building of evil spirits, as it was Mrs Uppingham's belief that the house was built over an abandoned mineshaft and that the spirits of miners who had been killed during a accident many years before were trapped or angry. All sorts of other theories were also produced, most of them fanciful and involving bad or trapped spirits. There is no doubt that there were indeed paranormal happenings in the house at Maxwell Park, but to blame all of them on the spirits of miners who may or may not have died somewhere in the vicinity would be foolish. It would seem in this case, as in so many others, that the people involved never looked to themselves for the answers. It always seems easier to involve disturbed souls who are held between two worlds.

Finally, the poltergeist activity stopped almost as suddenly as it had begun, when Ian Uppingham was sent away to live for a while with relatives in the north of Scotland, as by this point both Professor Roy and Rev. Magee had formed the firm opinion that he was the main focus of the phenomena. Although Professor Roy could not be sure that this course of action had cured the situation, everything did seem to become much quieter after it had been carried out.

Even in this very disturbing case, the investigators were of the opinion that the paranormal activity, however extreme, was not of another world, but caused by someone in this world.

I have a similar view about poltergeist activity, considering it almost the opposite of the ghost phenomenon, which is an emotional episode trapped in time and place, whereas a poltergeist is an explosion of emotion from deep within the mind of a person who is trying to imprison their own feelings. Such deep feelings tend to escape and build into a sort of telekinetic force that manifests around the troubled person.

Little Voice

So what do you do if you are faced with such a situation? Some people report these types of experiences to the Society for Psychical Research in Great Britain and in many other countries around the world. But not that many people know about the SPR, so let's face it, when it comes to ghostbusting, 'who are you gonna call?'

A large percentage of people who find themselves in this type of situation go to speak to a minister or priest, or even a medium or psychic. Our little Spiritualist church in Glasgow often had people asking for help with hauntings and other strange occurrences in their homes or places of work.

Mrs Primrose, the leader of our church, would attend any so-called disturbances of a paranormal nature when she could, but her first rule was that in such cases you must never work alone. First because you need verification if there really are paranormal phenomena taking place and secondly because as a medium, she would have to tune in and would need someone with her who would remain alert at all times. For these and other reasons, there were three of us, including Mrs P., at 33 The Crescent, back in 1993, to investigate a young couple's claims that their new home was haunted.

This very ordinary couple in their twenties lived in what looked like a very ordinary bungalow in the Glasgow area, except that they claimed that objects would move of their own accord, banging noises could be heard at all times of the day and night and that toys that belonged to their two-year-old daughter would move around frequently when no one was near them.

Mrs P. interviewed the couple one after the other. It was clear that both had witnessed the same phenomena, sometimes together and at other times individually. Both were clearly disturbed by what they had seen and heard and, what was worse, the wife was experiencing a sense of being held around her neck when she lay in bed.

Mrs P. was just about to tune in and see whether she could feel any spirit people when an ornament sitting on a low table began to turn and move towards the edge of the table, where it appeared to float for a moment before it landed softly on the carpet. Seconds afterwards, a small toy piano started to play by itself. Every one of us could see the small keys moving and hear the music, but there was no particular tune. The scene was bizarre, to say the least.

Then thumping sounds could be heard coming from around the bottom half of the living-room door and with this I heard a voice, a child's voice, saying, 'Mama'. I looked around at the others in the room to see their reactions and when no one mentioned it, I whispered to Mrs P. what I was hearing. Then everything stopped and at that moment I became aware of a small boy in the spirit world.

Mrs P. and I took the woman into the bedroom and Mrs P. asked me to tell her what I was sensing. As I did so, I sensed the child strongly again. I described him as being around 4 years old, having beautiful blond curls and big blue eyes and looking like a fit little boy of that age.

I then got the sense that he had died three years or so ago and that for some reason it was the young lady he was calling 'mama'. Her face was very red and she had tears running down the side of her cheeks, but she said nothing at this point. It was when I said that he wanted the toy elephant that she broke down sobbing. She explained to us that three years previously her little boy, who was just under a year old, had died due to a heart defect. This was eight months before she had met her husband. For one reason or another she had never mentioned to him that she had been in an earlier relationship and had lost her little boy. The only thing that she had kept to remind her of her son was a little toy elephant that lay on her pillow and that she held each night before going to sleep.

I'm sure the woman had her own reasons for not telling her new husband about her little boy, but it was clear to me that though she may have thought she had put him out of her mind, he was obviously not out of her heart and not out of her life either. All of the phenomena that were occurring in her home were consistent with the behaviour of a small child: objects being lifted from low tables, banging sounds coming from the floor or the bottom halves of the walls and doors, something wrapping itself round the woman's neck as she lay in bed and the toys often being moved or should I say 'played with'? It's bad enough when you can see the child lifting and moving things all over the place, but try to imagine how it would appear if an invisible child was causing the same disruption. I can see why the couple felt disturbed by the activities, but when they knew it was a child in the spirit world that was responsible, their view changed at once.

A week later Mrs P. received a letter from the young woman explaining that she had told her husband everything about the baby and her previous relationship. Apparently she had hoped she could block it all out of her mind, but her love for her lost child and the grief she had never allowed herself to feel had, it would seem, caused some of the psychic activity. When last I heard from the couple, which was quite recently, there had been no more disturbances in their home, except for the arrival of a new baby boy.

Attention Please

In cases of poltergeist activity there is usually somebody who is crying out for attention, either in the unseen world or this one.

One of the most famous cases of haunting in Britain was known as the Enfield Poltergeist. It started back in 1977 when a Mrs Peggy Harper, a divorcée in her mid-forties, was called by her daughter Janet, aged 11, and her son Pete, aged 10, to their bedroom where, they claimed, banging noises were keeping them awake.

Mrs Harper looked around the room for signs of anything that could cause the banging, but saw nothing untoward and left the room, closing the door behind her. No sooner had she done this than a loud banging sound echoed from the bedroom. When she re-entered, to her shock, a large set of drawers moved of its own accord some two feet from the wall and loud banging could be heard coming from the back wall, which adjoined the neighbour's house.

Mrs Harper removed both children from the bedroom and sent for her next-door neighbours, who also witnessed the moving of furniture and the banging sounds. Next the police were sent for. The police officers also heard the unexplained sounds and one officer even saw a chair inexplicably move across the floor and small plastic bricks and marbles being thrown around the room by some sort of invisible hand.

So intense were the phenomena that a minister was called for, then a local medium was brought in and finally the Society for Psychical Research. Morris Grose, a researcher for the SPR, attended this case for two years and witnessed all sorts of paranormal activity, from electrical faults and the unexplained mechanical failure of filming equipment to objects being hurled around rooms and bedclothes being mysteriously pulled off the children's beds. He even recorded voices speaking through the little girl, Janet. There were also reports of Janet levitating out of her bed; this scene was witnessed by one of the neighbours.

The case was widely reported and became the subject of TV programmes. At one point young Janet was taken to hospital for tests and while she was gone, for a period of six weeks, the phenomena stopped.

Some two years later, interest in the case began to fade and when this happened the psychic activity ceased. The investigators thought that the phenomena were somehow caused by Janet, as she seemed to be at the centre of all the activities and they had stopped when she wasn't around. Janet was one of four children being brought up by their mother on her own and therefore probably not a lot of attention was given to each child – again, a major factor in a case of poltergeist activity.

Poltergeist phenomena are usually associated with children or teenagers, often those starting puberty or starting menstruation, as Janet was in this case. It may be that the emotional changes and the build-up of intense feelings somehow cause telekinetic activity where objects move around and strange banging sounds are heard. All of this comes, I feel, from the child's need for attention or affection. Often the children involved in this type of case are said to be withdrawn or shy. Outwardly they may be quiet and calm, but inside there is emotional turbulence, which explodes as poltergeist activity when they crave attention.

The problem with cases of psychic phenomena involving children is that when a child is singled out as being the cause, even if the events were of a paranormal nature to begin with, there is always the chance that the child may invent more episodes to keep people interested.

Truths and Misconceptions about Poltergeists and Hauntings

- *If an object has moved a little from its original place in your home or you can't always find the things you are looking for, it must be a poltergeist.* Don't call the ghostbusters, it's probably just that you're becoming a wee bit forgetful. Real cases of poltergeist phenomena are very rare and, believe me, you would know if you had the real thing.

- *Loud banging sounds in your home mean it is haunted.* More often than not it's your central heating on the blink or there's some other rational explanation.

- *Children who behave badly and use foul language must be possessed.* They probably just watch too much late-night television or play too many violent computer games. Oh, never feed them pea soup before bed!

- *Hollywood movies portray hauntings in an accurate manner.* No, genuine cases of poltergeist-type hauntings don't feature A-list actors and don't tend to take place in houses built over ancient Indian burial grounds.

- *A poltergeist is an evil spirit.* It's far more likely to be telekinetic activity caused by a child suffering some deep emotional trauma.

- *Priests, ministers, psychical researchers or psychics should be called in immediately.* Most cases of poltergeist activity burn themselves out in a very short period of time. The less attention given to a poltergeist, the better – starving it of attention is the surest way to make it stop.

A Funny Thing Happened on the Way to the Haunting

Not all cases of poltergeist activity investigated by mediums and psychic researchers are as spectacular as that of the Enfield Poltergeist. Most of the cases I have gone to could be explained away using common sense and logic. One such case that I will never forget happened while I was visiting a Spiritualist church in England back in 1998.

I had just finished my demonstration of mediumship at around eight o'clock on the Sunday evening when the president of the church asked me if I would help him with an elderly lady who claimed to be having a terrible time with a spirit who she said was haunting her house and frightening her during the night. She lived just five minutes from the church, so I thought, *Why not?*

When we arrived at the house my mouth fell open at the sight that lay before me. The house looked as if a bomb had hit it. I thought, *This isn't poltergeists, it's terrorists*! However, I asked the elderly lady about the phenomena she had witnessed and she began to walk me into a sitting room where the furniture was falling to bits and claimed that she had seen the front of her sideboard fall off one day while she was having tea. This, she said, was her dead husband trying to make contact with her.

Then she took me to the kitchen where there was an old boiler fixed on the wall beside an open window. That boiler, she said, would go out regularly. I closed the window and sorted that 'ghost' out.

Then she said that the spirit had taken her husband's false teeth and other objects from her bathroom. It was at this point that I looked more closely at her mouth and realized that her husband might be closer to her than she knew, as the bottom denture she was wearing was continuously popping out of the right side of her mouth.

Finally she led us upstairs to the bedroom where she heard the sounds and voices of the spirits who kept her awake at night. I must admit that on entering the bedroom there were muffled noises from above the ceiling. 'Can you hear the voices?' she asked. What I could hear was the scratching and cooing of a bunch of pigeons in the attic.

I don't know if it was the mischievous side of my nature that overtook me then, but I gave the old lady a ritual that would expel the sounds in her room whenever she felt disturbed by them. I stood in the centre of the room and clapped my hands together with as much force as I could. Almighty thunder could be heard from above, followed by silence. I was going to follow this with the line from the film *Poltergeist*, when the medium, after ridding the family of the earthbound spirits, calls out, 'This house is clean!' but that would have been taking it too far.

As we left I couldn't help but think that there are more haunted people in the world than haunted houses.

Haunted People

Even though many buildings and places can give off an eerie feeling and I am sure many old houses and castles hold memories of their previous inhabitants' lives, loves, hates, passions and angers, I know, through the work that I do, that images of the past can only be accessed if the right conditions are present. It leaves me thinking that there is no such thing as a haunted place unless you have a living person involved. It's a bit like the old Chinese riddle: if a tree falls down in a forest, does it make a sound if there is no one there to hear it?

It's my opinion that *people* are haunted and that most of the phenomena they claim to experience take place in their own minds. I have witnessed many people who have sensed an eerie presence in an old building and then carried it into the realms of the ridiculous with their own imaginations. You only have to take certain psychics or mediums into an old castle and they start to visualize old soldiers, scenes of battle and murders, etc. To me, this is only due to imagination and association. A good medium who assists in a case of haunting should try to bring some peace of mind to the people who feel that their lives are being disturbed by such things. The last thing they need is to be told about gruesome murders and horrible tortures.

If someone has an overactive imagination, who knows what they can dream up, especially if they feel that they need attention from others around them? Cases of poltergeist activity are very rare, but many people tell stories of invisible presences in their homes or unexplained noises or objects being thrown violently around, only for it all to stop when the team of investigators arrives. Over the years it has become easier for me to tell the difference between a case of genuine paranormal activity and that of a person who needs attention and has invented a haunting to get it. But either way, something is not right and needs to be put right, whether the haunting is in the house or in the person's mind.

Mind over Psychic Matter

A case that illustrates this perfectly is that of a middle-aged woman who came to our Spiritualist church for help as she claimed that a spirit was having sexual intercourse with her in her sleep and that when she awoke she felt disgusted and violated.

This particular woman had lived by herself since her marriage had ended in divorce several years earlier. The phenomena began shortly after this, she said. At first she only felt a presence lying beside her, but as time passed it would overpower her and she would black out. When she awoke she would discover bruising around her thighs.

Mrs P. knew from the moment she heard this story that this was nothing to do with spirits, but she went along to the woman's house with another medium from the church and spent some time trying to sense whether there were any malevolent spirits around. After much discussion, she asked the woman if she would like to come to the church for spiritual healing and she insisted that she speak to her family doctor about the bruises and tell him her story.

The healers in our church gave this lady a lot of attention, compassion and much-needed friendship and the doctor referred her to a counsellor. No one encouraged the idea that a spirit was involved in what she had been experiencing, but many people offered to pray for her and within a month the experiences stopped. Sometimes all that is needed is for the person to find friendship and to be cared for by others.

The spirit world seems to get a lot of bad press when it comes to spooky happenings around people in this world. I suppose that for some people it is easier to blame the unseen than to lay the blame at your own door.

Opening the Dark Rooms

When I see people afraid of the unseen world it bothers me, because I know that there is nothing to be afraid of. With all the different experiences I have had in what people would consider the frightening world of ghosts, spirits and haunted places, what I find lies at the heart of such things is fear, the fear that everyone has in the dark rooms of their minds, those little compartments we push all our fears and phobias into in the hope that we don't have to open the door on them ever again. In everyday life we can forget about them, but when we feel alone or emotionally vulnerable, they float up to our conscious mind and remind us that we have issues to deal with and fears to face.

As a medium I have, as part of my development, had to explore the dark rooms where fear hides and face it and conquer it. This is why I have no fear of things that go bump in the night. Neither do I have any fear of dying, nor of what comes after that. Part of my journey is about exorcising my own demons, realizing my weaknesses, accepting them and letting them go. As long as I do this type of self-investigation, I will never feel haunted in my home, my life or in my mind.

Anyone can rid themselves of the fears which haunt the dark rooms of their mind by illuminating the hidden corners with the light of knowledge. Even when you are faced with episodes of paranormal activity that defy all logic, there is still no need to invite fear into your mind.

In any case, many events which have no rational explanation are actually intriguing and miraculous.

CHAPTER SIX

Public Non-Reality

Public Non-Reality

At the end of October 2001 my son Steven, who had just turned 17, went off to join the Royal Navy. He had just started his first week of training at HMS *Raleigh* in Cornwall when I underwent what was to become one of the strangest episodes of my adult life.

Each Sunday I walked my dog, Charlie, in the old cemetery close to where I lived. The Sunday after Steven left for the navy, my friend Jim and I walked Charlie together. Charlie is an English springer spaniel, the type of dog that likes to run wild through undergrowth and bushes, chasing anything that moves. This particular day he disappeared and was out of sight for about five minutes before Jim and I began to call his name and whistle for him to come back to us. Instead of Charlie's usual response, which would be to come panting through bushes carrying a stick or stone, we could hear him barking as if he was in some sort of distress.

We made our way towards the sound and found ourselves in a very old part of the cemetery, where I had never been before. Charlie was sitting in front of an old headstone, barking repeatedly. As I got closer I noticed the name on the headstone and was shocked at what I saw: it was the grave of a man called Gordon Smith, who was a writer, and his son, Steven Andrew Smith, able seaman, who had died at sea during World War I. Neither Jim nor I could believe the coincidence, even down to the Andrew, which is my son's middle name. I must say it felt very strange to look at this old grave, even though it dated back almost 100 years.

Six weeks after going into the Royal Navy Steven decided that he wanted to leave; he simply felt that it was not the life for him. I never mentioned the gravestone to him, nor did I go back to the old part of the cemetery. It wasn't until February 2004 that I happened to be walking through the cemetery with Jim and Charlie and we decided we would walk back up to the old part to see the grave which had spooked us so much two and a half years earlier.

It was what we didn't see this time that was really spooky. The stone still read 'Gordon Smith, Writer', but there was absolutely no mention of Steven Andrew or for that matter any son at all. The only other name on the headstone was that of a daughter Daphne, who had died in the 1920s. For the second time Jim and I were staring at this headstone, unable to believe what we were seeing. I could think of no way in which this old granite stone could have been physically changed in this way without some sign of deterioration or damage to the granite.

Had this happened to me when I was on my own I would have put the whole episode down to my imagination, but the fact that my friend witnessed the same thing on each occasion made me wonder what was going on.

Who can explain such strange events? I simply call them 'public non-reality', a term for the supernatural episodes in life which may never be explained. I think of public non-reality whenever I come across cases where more than one person has witnessed strange phenomena which defy our physical laws and have no rational explanation.

Spirits Lifting

Albert Best was the sort of medium who never had to exaggerate his gifts – normally, what he did spoke for itself. But when I was helping a friend to research his life for a book, I did uncover an incredible example of public non-reality which involved him. This account was given to me by a Catholic priest who lives just outside Glasgow.

I was invited, along with some friends of mine who had joined together to form an ecumenical group to study and discuss religious matters, to attend a session of mediumship given by the late Mr Albert Best. The group met in Glasgow at the home of my friend who was hosting this session. I had been told by several members of the group who were familiar with the medium and his work that he could be quite phenomenal, but none of us could have ever expected what we were about to see.

Albert Best was a man small in stature, who appeared, in my view, very shy. He seemed to be intimidated by the gathering of men and women in our group who were of either of a religious or scientific background. Soon after the formal introductions, Mr Best sat in a large and very heavy-looking armchair at the far end of the well-lit sitting room, whilst the rest of us were seated around the room in a sort of circle formation. Mr Best closed his eyes and fell into a sort of trance and a voice spoke through him in an accent which was hard to distinguish as any exact nationality. He began to give what I believe was a message from a spirit on the other side to one of my colleagues, who was confirming what he was hearing when, without any warning, the chair on which Mr Best was sitting began to shake furiously. Mr Best snapped out of his trance state and began to protest to unseen forces around him, saying, 'Stop that!' and 'Put me down!'.

If I had not been in the company of people whom I consider sane of mind, I would not have believed my eyes, as the chair, along with Mr Best, lifted up till the little man's head was near ceiling height. No sooner had this happened than voices could be heard, which I can say came from no one seen sitting in that room. The chair slowly returned to the floor with Mr Best still calling out to the invisible forces around him and the session ended soon after. The medium explained that he was unharmed and never in any danger, but he did not like it when they played games like that just to impress people. He said that the spirits who had played this prank on him were men who had been part of his squadron during the war and who had died in Africa in 1943. This was Mr Best's account; quite honestly, I, along with the most of my group, even those among us with a background in physics, have absolutely no explanation for what we experienced.

Albert Best was not the only medium to levitate in the presence of such notable company. The most famous medium of the Victorian era, Daniel Douglas Home (pronounced Hume), was reported to have levitated many times. Many great men of science witnessed him floating in the air while making heavy items of furniture around him float at the same time. His feats of levitation happened not once, but hundreds of times in well-lit rooms.

Even though D. D. Home's amazing powers were tested in so many ways, by so many people, he was never seriously accused of fraud. He even astounded the physicist Sir William Crookes, who wrote favourably about Home's levitational abilities in *The Quarterly Journal of Science* in 1871. Crookes said that he could not conclude anything other than the humanly impossible had happened.

D. D. Home's explanation for the phenomena was the same as Albert Best's – that spirits he knew would lift him and gently glide him around a room, never bringing harm to himself or any other person concerned. The spirits, he would say, were demonstrating their powers to convince people of a spirit life beyond our physical world.

Flyer Tuck

It is not only mediums who have been seen to fly by members of the public. Joseph of Copertino, known in his lifetime as 'the flying monk' and later St Joseph, was seen flying on many occasions. He was born in Apulia, Italy, in 1603 and at the age of 21 became a Franciscan priest in the Order of Conventuals near Copertino. He had a reputation for starving and flagellating himself so much that people soon thought of him as holy. One day during prayers and mass in the chapel, he floated up over the other monks and landed gently on the altar in a state of ecstasy. Even though he flew directly over the many candles, he was not burned, nor were his robes singed. After many such episodes he was sent to see the Pope in Rome. Once again he floated off the ground and rose high into the air in a state of ecstasy.

Eventually one of his superiors became very hostile towards him and decided to chastise and humiliate him and while under this superior his flights stopped for almost two years. His ability to fly returned when he was allowed to visit Rome again. When the people gave him an enthusiastic welcome, he flew more than 15 yards to embrace the statue of the Virgin on the altar.

St Joseph made no claim for a miraculous or divine reason for his flights. All he needed, he said, was a feeling of deep joy. For the rest of his life he would experience these flights and even when he was close to death his doctor reported that he was levitating six inches from his bed as he reported the sounds and scents of Paradise waiting for him.

Joseph of Copertino was canonized just over 100 years after his death when the Pope ordered an investigation into his flights and found they were backed up by hundreds of depositions.

I don't know about anyone else, but I certainly think that to see a monk fly would be a good enough reason to attend church. But then the Lord does work in mysterious ways.

The Nature of Miracles

Who can say why certain miraculous events happen? And why don't we look more closely at the causes of such supernatural occurrences when they do happen? For years people have reported unbelievable happenings like crying statues, apparitions of religious or holy figures or even flying monks for that matter. Do we accept the miraculous only as long as it lies in the past and concerns gurus, saints and messiahs? Are we afraid to see it as evidence of the fantastic nature of the human spirit?

We only have to look at the life of Jesus Christ. Do we actually believe that he walked on water or turned water into wine or healed the sick or are these seen as fables created to give us hope and faith? What about Saint Bernadette's vision of the Virgin Mary at Lourdes and the many other people who swear that they have witnessed such visions – can they all be put down to imagination or self-delusion?

My own opinion is that all forms of public non-reality are caused by people who, whether they are aware of it or not, are allowing more of their superconscious mind to encroach on their earthly mind. This superconsciousness is the spiritual being which emanates a small fraction of itself into human form and in its more complete form connects us to the higher, more spiritual realms of life. It is only because people tend not to believe that they are much more than just people in the physical world that they find the supernatural hard to accept.

Miracles are no more than glimpses of other dimensions of the human consciousness which, when they break into physical reality, distort our normal idea of life in such a way that we are faced with the unbelievable or unexplainable. This may change our view of reality and expand our consciousness. After all, weren't most of our religions founded by miraculous people who were teaching us about our spiritual nature?

The development of consciousness has allowed certain Buddhist monks, lamas and yogis to practise feats of mind over matter like sitting in sub-zero temperatures and yet still producing enough body heat to dry a wet blanket within seconds. Others have been known to cover vast distances on foot in times which are not humanly possible, while others have been seen in more than one location at the same time. This type of yogic practice has been going on for thousands of years and even today there are many yogis who can perform such feats. How is this possible? It may be called mind over matter, but what does that mean?

In order for there to be any form of miraculous event, there has to be a life form to instigate it. When visions appear to people, it is because they are allowing their own spiritual energy to be manipulated in order for the phenomena to occur, as most of these types of visions are projected through the mind of the person who experiences them. The same thing applies to most supernatural experiences.

Truths and Misconceptions about Public Non-Reality

- *Miracles happen just because you want them to.* The truth is that even if you pray lots and lots, it still guarantees you nothing.
- *If a famous saint or holy person has witnessed a miraculous vision at a certain site, you can too.* No, it's not likely, even if you make a pilgrimage to it.
- *Most people who cause supernatural phenomena to occur do so deliberately.* In fact most don't know they have done it at all and very few such miracle workers could produce a repeat performance.
- *Superhuman beings can produce gifts from the higher realms out of thin air for their devotees.* This often just reeks of a scam to recruit new members to their cult.
- *Statues can cry tears from Heaven.* Check the roof they are under for leaks!
- *The world is full of miracles.* It is, but most of them are natural phenomena.

Faces in the Floor

In the early 1990s I was working as a medium in Spain. I happened to be hosted by Ray and June Smith, who were members of the Gibraltar Society for Psychical Research. On a day off, Ray asked if I would like to look at a videotape of one of the more fascinating cases he had investigated.

The film began with Ray entering a small house in a Spanish village called Belmez in the Sierra Nevada mountains. Inside he was introduced to a small elderly Spanish woman named Maria Gomez Pereira, who led him into her kitchen. As the video recorder was pointed to the floor I was astonished to see many faces. I first thought these had been painted or sketched by an artist, but it turns out that they had been appearing on Maria Gomez Pereira's kitchen floor since 1971.

When the first face appeared, a man's face, Maria and her family decided to have the cement slab lifted and a new one laid in its place. In just two weeks a second face had appeared in the same place as before. Again the family wanted to remove the slab. At this point the mayor of Belmez stepped in and had the slabs with faces preserved. It was decided that the floor should be excavated as there were stories that the house had been built on an old graveyard. Some human bones were found and were given a proper burial in the hope that this would put an end to the strange episode. Once again a new cement floor was laid, only this time more faces appeared, not only a man's face this time but also the face of a woman and many other smaller faces of different people surrounding her.

By now Maria Gomez's house was attracting the attention of all sorts of investigators and scientists. Some even tested the cement floors which had previously been removed for signs of paints and charcoals, but none were found. One team of scientists left cameras recording over a period of weeks and the film showed clearly that faces were appearing from the floor as if by magic. Some would come and stay, while others would come and go.

Ray's video shows many faces – men, women and children of all ages and all expressions. As I watched, I got the feeling that Maria was the cause of the phenomenon. Her emotions, I felt, affected the expressions on the faces. It is my feeling that when someone discovers such things, they themselves have given emotional energy to them and more often than not, one person is responsible for this sort of phenomenon. If they are not around, nothing happens.

The faces are still appearing on the floor of Maria's house and I feel that they won't stop until Maria herself is no longer there. But after more than 20 years, scientists and psychical researchers have come no closer to finding an explanation for the faces on the floor.

More to Us than Meets the Eye

The unseen energy that flows around us has much more to do with public non-reality than we know. On one occasion I was giving a message from a man in the spirit world to his wife in a private sitting when he told me to tell her that he always gave her a red rose on Valentine's Day. No sooner had I mentioned this to her than a red rose from a vase on her table lifted up by itself and landed on her lap. In her eyes this was some kind of miracle, but as a medium I knew that the spirit of her husband had used my energy to do this, as during the transporting of the rose from one place to the other, I felt a dullness run through my body, as though someone had put their hand into my stomach and removed something. Energy had to be taken from me to allow the moving of the flower.

Supernatural events in this world are all created out of the energies in and around us. Even when a person sees an apparition, the spirit is using the person's energy in order to appear physical again. This may explain the strange sensation people get at such times – quite apart from the shock of the whole episode, there is also a draw on the person's energy field. In cases where mediums are used to enable spirits to appear in a physical way, the medium will feel a pull on their own energy, just as I did when the rose was being transported. It's only because a medium is more acquainted with the more subtle energies than the average person that they don't consider the experience to be strange at all.

Not All There

For years mediums have produced a physical phenomenon known as materialization, which allows the spirit to reproduce their own physical image by using the life force of the medium they are working with. This type of mediumship was at its height from Victorian times to the Second World War and thousands of people witnessed their loved ones rematerialized at séances and were able to speak to them in person, as it were, in this solid form.

In order for this type of mediumship to take place the medium would usually have to go into a very deep trance in which their bodily functions would slow to almost a standstill. This was required in order for the spirit to use the life energy of the medium to mould their own image and for a period of time come back into the physical dimension.

The effect on the medium was to be left depleted of energy after the séance. Even others sitting at the séance would feel drained, as physical energy would often be taken from some of them as well to sustain the materialization.

At one séance the aunt of one young man came through and spoke to her relative for almost half an hour. It was only when she lifted the gown that she appeared to be wearing that it was realized that she was only half materialized from the waist up. She said there was not enough energy to reproduce her entire body. Nonetheless, she told her nephew that she had come to speak to him, so did not require her legs to do this. At other séances hands or just faces would appear, because the energy from the group and the medium combined was not strong enough to allow a full materialization to take place.

Over many years, through many mediums, thousands of people witnessed spirits becoming solid forms and conversing with their loved ones, if only for a short time. There are thousands of testimonies, infra-red photographs and voice recordings, many authenticated by doctors, scientists, politicians and others we would have to consider to be of sane mind, not to mention the masses who saw and conversed with loved ones, whom we would think they would recognize. Yet no matter how many times this type of manifestation took place, there were always objections and claims of fraud and skulduggery from the sceptics. Some of *their* claims were founded, though many other cases which were tried and tested and defied the law of physics will simply lie in files as unexplained mysteries. If nothing else, there was always a great deal of controversy going on in the old séance rooms, some of which even made headline news.

The Last Witch

A medium who certainly made the headlines in Britain back in 1944 was the famous materialization medium Helen Duncan. Her mediumship became a great talking point after she gave a séance in Portsmouth in January 1944 when a young sailor materialized in solid form and spoke to his mother, telling her that he had been killed when his ship the HMS *Barham* had been sunk. He went on to mention that a great many of his shipmates had been killed and were with him on the other side. He also told his mother that she would not receive conformation of his death from the War Office for another three weeks.

Can you imagine what it felt like for that mother to see her son appear to her in this way? So strong was her belief in what had happened at the séance that she immediately contacted the Admiralty, asking them for conformation of the sinking of the HMS *Barham*. She was not given it, but instead was visited by two senior Admiralty officials who questioned her about the information she had on the sinking of the ship. She told them about the séance and then heard nothing more about the matter until three weeks later, when she was, as her son had told her, given confirmation of his death due to the sinking of his ship.

Meanwhile, in Helen Duncan's next séance, her spirit guide made an appearance and asked the people who were responsible for running the séances in the Portsmouth Spiritualist church to beware of naval officers attending future séances. He warned that they must not be allowed in or they would bring great harm to his medium.

It would appear that no one at the church paid any attention to this warning, as later that month, at a séance again held in the Portsmouth, Helen had just gone into a state of trance and started emanating ectoplasm from her solar plexus when two naval officers and an undercover policeman suddenly jumped to their feet, put on the lights and called out 'Police!', at which point the door was kicked in by other police officers who made a grab for the ectoplasm, saying that it was cotton sheets.

Before going into a trance, Helen Duncan always insisted on being searched by members of the group, which ruled out any fraudulence. As well as the search, she would strip down to her underwear and put on a thin robe which anyone could examine before she began to work. After that, no one would interfere with her in any way, as to do so when she was in a trance could be very damaging to her. So when the police seized her, she came out of the trance in a terrible state and no one who was attending the séance could help her. Helen's body was badly burned around the stomach and solar plexus and she was in a state of shock as she and the leaders of the church were arrested and taken into police custody.

The medium was kept in prison for three months, without any chance of bail, until her trial, which was held at the Old Bailey in London in April 1944. At the Old Bailey, she was tried under the Witchcraft Act of 1735 and unbelievably sentenced to nine months in Holloway prison for demonstrating her mediumship, as there was no evidence that she had cheated. The people attending the séance had asked to be thoroughly searched, but inexplicably, the police had refused. To this day no one can understand either why the medium was held in prison for such a long time with no chance of bail. It would seem to me that someone wanted her out of the way so she could not give the public any more official war secrets.

Medium Rare

The kind of phenomena produced by mediums like Helen Duncan and many other amazing mediums of the past must have been the most convincing evidence that there was truly a life after death. The sad reality about that type of mediumship was that it did lend itself to fraudulence and I'm sure that many people did fake séances to make money out of the bereaved.

I never got to see Helen Duncan's mediumship, as she died in 1956, but my old teacher Mrs Primrose once gave me a fascinating account of one of the many times that she witnessed Helen's amazing mediumship.

Mrs P. told me how she and a friend helped to search Helen before the séance and that all she was wearing was a pair of gym knickers under a flimsy black robe. After the search the medium was taken to a seat where her hands and feet were bound to an armchair which was placed behind a black curtain at the corner of the séance room. All the lights were switched off and a dim red lit was set in front of the black curtain. Minutes after the red light came on, a white mist could be seen by the whole group of 16 people sitting in the seats in a circle around the room. This ectoplasm grew thicker and began to take the form of a tall man who stood, Mrs P. said, about six foot tall, much taller than Helen. He spoke to the group, telling them that he was called Albert and was Helen's guide and he would help bring through the spirits who wanted to communicate.

Mrs P. described how 10 different spirits materialized one after the other. All of them were recognized by their families and friends. One little girl of about 4 years of age ran to her mother and hugged her, saying that she was all right now and that she wasn't to cry any more. Mrs P. also had a message at that séance from one of her old neighbours, who asked her to pass on a message to her husband, whom she said Mrs P. would meet the following day. She asked her not to be shocked when she met him, as he had had his right leg amputated since she last saw him.

At the close of the séance Helen was untied and allowed to dress and then she came and spoke the group, asking them if they had received any good messages, as she had been in such a deep trance that she had no knowledge of the proceedings.

My teacher was a medium herself and a person who I'm certain would be able to detect fraud in a second and in this case she felt sure that the incredible phenomena were quite genuine. The following evening, in her own church, she saw the husband of the spirit neighbour who had asked her to pass on the message. He was sitting in the back row of the church and as Mrs P. went towards to him, he stood up to greet her, saying, 'It's been a long time, Jean'. She says that her mouth fell open when she realized that, just as his wife had said, his right leg was missing. This was further proof, not that she needed it after witnessing the full materialization of 10 spirit people the previous evening.

Both during and after her life Helen Duncan was the subject of many investigations, with a variety of conclusions being drawn about her mediumship. A number of books have been written about her, some of which are listed in the Further Reading section, and anyone interested in her life should have no problem finding further information.

Unbelievable but True

Many people have claimed to have witnessed miracles and other unbelievable events that defy natural laws as we understand them. There are masses of accounts of physical phenomena and miraculous occurrences of public non-reality held in the Society for Psychical Research in London and other bodies and religious groups around the world, filled under 'Unexplained'. Even though there is often no explanation for certain cases, this doesn't mean that the events haven't happened, only that there is no rational explanation for them. As a medium I encounter many people who tell me about episodes of public non-reality, yet I'm never shocked or surprised by them. Even the more unbelievable may turn out to be true and to have meaning.

It is all too easy to dismiss such claims, but we can often see their effects in the lives of the people affected. Episodes of public non-reality will often cause the witness to rethink their life and expand their consciousness in a spiritual way. They can tear down the boundaries of the mind and broaden their horizons, bringing an awareness of the true power of consciousness. When our conscious mind is ready to accommodate supernatural occurrences, then the so-called miraculous will be considered the norm.

CHAPTER SEVEN

Altered States

Altered States

I was 11 years old and travelling on a train with my parents and two of my older brothers when I first experienced something very strange. We had been visiting my mother's brother over the Easter holidays in London and were on our homeward journey, which at that time took eight hours. I had been given a new watch by my Uncle Mick, which kept me quiet for a while, except for telling everyone that another minute had passed. It was going to be a very long journey.

My brothers seemed to pass their time better than I did, by reading and drawing, only interrupting my parents' conversation now and then to ask, 'How long to go?'.

I had by now become fascinated by the second hand on my watch and was transfixed watching it go round. Then I became aware of the light in the compartment changing from its usual yellowy-whitish glow to a very dull, almost sepia colour, while the smoke from my mother's cigarette was turning from a silvery mist into an amazing orange colour. My family looked like negatives of themselves. My head was down, looking at my wrist on the small table just under the large window, but somehow I was also standing in a room which was familiar to me. I was watching my best friend, Alex, who lived next door to me in Glasgow, standing over a bed where his mother lay looking very sick indeed. I could hear his mother say, 'That's enough now,' and Alex was led out of the room by someone taller than he was.

In the compartment of the train my mother was asking me what I was looking at and forcing me to answer her, my brothers were making up funny songs and my father was half asleep with his head hanging to one side. Yet I could still see Alex, who was holding a large Easter egg in his hands, only now he was in a dim sepia-coloured light and his father was telling him not to cry.

'What are you staring at?' my mother shouted.

'My watch,' I answered slowly. 'It's six o'clock.' We were halfway through our journey.

Now I was totally back with my family on the train. Soon afterwards I fell asleep. I remember my father waking me to tell me we had arrived in Glasgow. It was just after 10 o'clock. I slept again on the short journey from the train station to our house and was put to bed, still asleep, by my father.

The following morning I wanted to go next door to Alex's house with a gift I had bought him in London, but my mother said I shouldn't go. She explained to me that Alex's mother had died and I should wait till another time to give him his gift.

I saw Alex just after his mother's funeral and he told me that he had seen her just before she died and she had given him an Easter egg, which he would keep forever. I asked him what time she had died and he said he didn't know exactly, but he had seen her at six o'clock. He knew this because his sister had arrived just before six; she had been asked to look after him.

Looking back at this experience I can see a similarity to what is known as remote viewing, where a psychic can be in one place and focus their mind on an event taking place somewhere else. Distance does not limit this type of psychic vision. I can also liken it to astral travel, where the mind can be projected to other places and bring back information. In both remote viewing and astral projection, a person can hone their skill to choose where they wish to go.

For me this was the beginning of what I now know to be trance mediumship, where my mind 'moves out' to allow a spirit being to use my mind and body to communicate with their loved ones.

The Meditative Mind

I'm sure that many people would say that I am not in possession of my full mind anyway, especially when I try to describe some of my early experiences. In fact, from an early age, I tried to dismiss some of the more bizarre events myself, putting them down to childish fantasies and daydreams. I even wondered if I had made them up to get attention, but most of them contained information that was intelligent, true and beyond my knowledge.

I very rarely mentioned my experiences at all after the reaction I got from my mother the first time I saw a materialized spirit and had an intelligent conversation with him. All I can say is she sent me out of the house in a hurry. It was only when I joined a spiritual development class in my twenties that I began to make sense of what was really happening to me in my child-hood. A big part of my development was to clear my mind through meditation, look at myself and my life in a rational and fully focused way and try to understand my mind.

The reason that any medium has to learn to understand their own mind is so that they can distinguish the difference between their own thoughts and any telepathic communications or psychic images from another source.

Meditation helps to ground you and practising it on a regular basis helps you to be more in control of how you think. It may even help you to control your actions and shape your attitude in a much better way.

Even though I started out as a good meditator and had no problem in focusing my mind, grounding myself in reality and breathing well, I began to notice, now and then, that when my mind became clear and still, either with my eyes closed or open, I would experience a change of light and tone around me. Often when this would occur I would sense my awareness separating into two parts and while being able to stay in the moment, I would find that I would be equally aware of being somewhere else and could describe, in full detail, both situations.

My teacher, Mrs Primrose, never saw this as a problem; she would often comment that I was a natural medium and that this type of thing would happen from time to time. She told me to keep a record to see if there appeared to be a pattern to this separating of consciousness. I was to record which time frame I found myself in and check out, where possible, if the scenes I was observing could be validated by anyone else.

Mrs P. told me that I was what was known as a 'trance medium' and that not only could I receive messages in my mind from the other side, what is known as mental mediumship, but I could also enter a trance and allow my mind and body to be used by a spirit person for more direct communication. However, I would have to learn to discipline my mind and control this sort of mediumship or, if I did not wish to be used like this, I would have to learn to close down this area of my mind and focus on my mental mediumship.

I decided to learn more about trance mediumship.

Coming Through

One of the great exponents of trance mediumship was the man who became a great friend and mentor to me, Albert Best. Albert was very understated about what he did, but when I was working for the Gibraltar Society for Psychical Research I found a videotape of him carrying out spiritual healing on a woman who had a large painful lump protruding from her neck. Albert, in a trance, could be seen standing beside the woman moving his hands slowly over the neck area, his hands about an inch from her body. A moment later a voice could be heard speaking through him in a foreign language. The woman responded in the same language, but with a look of surprise on her face. The unbelievable thing about this was that the language was Mandarin. Seconds later, again unbelievably, the lump disappeared completely. The patient was reduced to tears of joy, while Albert shook his head, opened his eyes, lit up a cigarette and chatted in English to the psychical researchers who were monitoring the situation as if nothing unusual had happened.

When I later asked Albert about this episode and how he was able to speak in another language, he explained that whenever he gave healing a spirit guide would come through him or 'overshadow' him. This meant that Albert's conscious mind was displaced and the spirit guide could work through him, enabling the spirit performing the healing to have better use of his body. On this occasion, where the patient understood the guide's own language, he could use Albert's voice to speak as he would have when alive in the physical world.

Incidentally, Mr Best normally spoke in an accent which was a mixture of Glaswegian and his native Irish, which made it difficult for people to understand his English, let alone a foreign language.

Mind Control

What Albert had been practising in this case was a variation of controlled trance mediumship. This form of trance mediumship is so called because the spirit guide of the entranced medium uses the medium's voice to pass messages from the spirit world, rather than sending mental images through the medium's mind.

One of the mediums Albert looked up to as a great exponent of controlled trance was a woman called Helen Hughes, whose work during the Second World War was revered by Spiritualists and who had a huge public following in Britain and other countries. Sometimes as many as 2,000 people would pack halls around the UK to witness Mrs Hughes demonstrate her amazing gift.

Like Albert Best, Helen Hughes was known for her public mediumship more than her trance mediumship, but those who experienced this amazing medium in an altered state became convinced that spirit people were actually controlling her voice. Many people who witnessed her work also testified that the spirit person who was speaking through her would often be seen transfiguring her face.

I spoke to a lady from India who, back in the early 1960s, had a sitting with Helen Hughes while visiting the UK. It was not something she had planned and she had not been interested in the subject of life after death when she had been introduced to Helen, but nevertheless she asked her if she would try to make a contact with the other side for her. The private sitting was recorded and as I listened to the tape I thought of how much I still had to learn to reach the level of mediumship demonstrated by Helen Hughes or Albert Best.

On the tape Helen begins talking normally, explaining what may or may not happen during the sitting. The Indian woman can be heard answering politely. Then Helen claims to make contact with her grandmother who is in the spirit world and within a short space of time is speaking in a completely different voice and one of the Indian languages. Even now the sitter cannot believe what happened. The details given could only have come from her grandmother, who had died some years earlier. She even used a pet name that her grandmother alone had used for her as a child.

As a result of this sitting Helen Hughes was invited to work in India. There are a great many reports and taped evidence from her time there to prove that on many occasions she channelled the spirits of Indian people who spoke through her in their own native tongue. Helen herself was never, to anyone's knowledge, able to speak any foreign language.

Out of my Mind

As I progressed in my development group, I began to notice the different stages of trance. My conscious mind separating to be in two places at once was only the beginning. Once I learned to accept that this was a way to intensify my abilities as a medium, I relaxed and allowed the spirit who had been one of my guides from my early childhood to take me through each step as it came to me. Mrs P. was always there to give me answers when I was unsure and by now I had become friendly with Albert Best, who also took an interest in how my mediumship was progressing.

It was around this time that I experienced my first deep trance, during which I was controlled by a spirit person who wanted to communicate with Mrs P. The feeling was so overwhelming that I don't have much recall of what happened, but Mrs P. told me later that the message which was given through me might help someone she knew who was in a lot of trouble. I can see now that this message was so important that any interference from my mind might have distorted it, so the spirit person decided to put me into a state of deep trance. Though I remembered nothing of what happened, the experience felt so amazing that I wanted to learn more about it.

Soon I was able to stay alert and feel each change that my body and mind went through in order to allow my spirit guide to forge a strong link with me. First I would feel my mind expanding in a way that allowed me to be aware of what was happening around me and what was happening to others who were sitting nearby. Then I would feel a pulse or rhythmic vibration in the room itself, as if all of the empty space between every person or object was alive and breathing. There were times when I would hear people thinking. At this point my body would feel as if it were shutting down organ by organ until all I was aware of was my heart beating more and more slowly, like a metronome slowing almost to a stop. This was the point at which I blacked out the first time I went through this experience, but when I learned to go beyond this sensation I could actually feel the spirit people around me. They seemed more physical to me than the people who were alive and in the room with me.

It took me years to allow my mind to open up to this level, even though I was a natural-born medium. Each time I sat in my group I would learn to let go a little bit more and clear out more of the emotional garbage which I had allowed to clutter my mind for years and which can distort spirit communication. Part of the discipline of development is to learn not to become affected emotionally but to remain still when all in your mind is in motion.

There came a point when I could sit in this state and speak clearly to the spirit people the way I had done as a child, before my mind had been conditioned by fear and emotional pain. Now I knew for certain that I was able to move out of my emotional mind and experience for a short time my own spirit linking and conversing with others. During this time I would feel the presence of my spirit guide moving closer to me until I was engulfed by the warm loving sensation of being held in a beautiful state of grace by a highly evolved being of light.

It was when my consciousness had moved away and my guide had filled the space that was left that he would use my voice to speak to the other people in the room, often giving them messages from spirit people they had lost and at other times speaking to them directly and answering any questions they had about the afterlife. He said that he had lived many years ago in China, that he was a man of no great importance and that any wisdom he had had come through observing nature. His intention, he said, was to help people to understand compassion and lose their fear of living. It is often said that with spirit guides and their mediums like attracts like, but I think he made a mistake in choosing me to work through!

The more I practised this type of trance mediumship, the stronger my own abilities as a mental medium became. Now when I work in public I have a sense of my guide slightly overshadowing me. Nothing has convinced me more that we are spirit and live beyond this physical realm than the experience of being beyond my mind in a state of trance where the spirit people are so real that I can touch them, and it's this understanding that has given me trust in what I do.

Truths and Misconceptions about Trance

- *Mediums who go into a trance make moaning sounds and gyrate their bodies in circles before speaking in a loud exaggerated voice.* Yes, they do – when they're hamming it up!
- *Trance mediums sit in darkened rooms by candlelight listening to whale sounds on a tape recorder.* They can – but it doesn't help!
- *Spirit guides speak through trance mediums to spout hellfire and brimstone or to predict the end of the world.* There is normally a good reason why they have made the effort to communicate in this fashion, but it's usually not apocalyptic.
- *A real experience of trance will leave the medium exhausted.* This shouldn't be the case – it should fill them with spiritual energy and vitality. They should be radiant at the end of it.
- *Cleopatra, Jesus Christ and other well-known figures pop in regularly to communicate.* This is usually just

wishful thinking on the part of the so-called medium.

- *All you need to do to go into a trance is to close your eyes and speak in a different voice.* This is just not true! So use your common sense to assess what you have heard and the reason why it was said. And don't believe everything that you hear.

Big Woman, Deep Trance

The funny thing about a medium going into a trance and speaking in a different voice is that it is funny. I mean funny peculiar, not funny ha, ha. Although one story comes to mind which I always share with students who wish to learn about deep trance mediumship.

It happened back in the late 1960s in Glasgow to a woman I shall call Joan for the purposes of this story. Joan went along to a Spiritualist church as she had become interested in the subject and felt that she was a bit psychic herself, and she was quite surprised to receive a message from the medium on her first visit. The medium told Joan that she was indeed psychic and should learn to develop her gift in a development class. After the service finished she gave her the name and address of a woman she should go to to develop her gift.

Joan arrived at the house the following Thursday evening. Standing outside the front door she felt a little apprehensive, but eventually she knocked on the door, which opened almost at once and there stood a very frail-looking elderly lady. Joan thought she must be the medium who would train her, but the little lady told her that she was only there to make tea for all of the people who sat together in the group. She showed Jean into the front room of the house. About 10 people were sitting in a circular formation and there was one empty chair, which Joan was ushered towards by a very large, roundly built lady who called out, 'Ah, you must be Joan. Come and sit by me and when we are all ready we shall begin to meditate'.

Joan sat down and wondered, 'How do you meditate?'. No one explained what to do and she was too scared to ask, so she just closed her eyes and thought about anything she could for the next half-hour.

Finally the large lady beside her called out in a loud voice, 'Stop meditating now and tell me what you witnessed during your meditation'.

Joan panicked as she had only thought about things that

she had to do at home, but as they went round the group and she listened to some of the rubbish being spoken, she decided to copy them and say she was off on a spiritual journey.

'Joan, tell me what happened to you now,' demanded the big lady.

'I saw an Indian gentleman dressed in lots of feathers,' Joan lied.

'An Indian in feathers! Well, I shall expect great things from you in the future,' the big lady said.

She then explained to the group that she was about to go into a very deep trance and that she required everyone to be completely silent as she could be injured or even killed if any member of the group moved or made a sound.

Joan sat holding her breath, watching the big lady gyrating and wobbling. With the weird sounds she was making, it seemed as though she was having a fit. Then, without warning, she jumped to her feet, hands outstretched, and started to talk in a very forced deep voice. 'Welcome, earthlings! I come from the planet Uranus and I come to give you advice about your planet.'

Joan's eyes almost popped out of their sockets. Then at that very moment this gem of trance philosophy was interrupted by the door opening slowly. For a moment Joan was afraid of what might be coming in, but it turned out to be the old tea lady, who paid no attention to the big lady in the trance and went around the circle of people asking what they would like on their sandwiches. Joan watched her slowly make her way around the group until she stopped behind the big medium and whispered, 'What would you like on your sandwiches, cheese or ham?'.

As quick as a flash the big lady's head turned and she broke her trance for a second and shouted loudly, 'Ham!' and then went immediately back to giving the 'earthlings' a dressing down for ruining their planet!

For some reason, Joan never went back to that development group after that night.

A Famous Trance

That message from Uranus might not have had much of an impact on the world, but back in the 1960s a medium from London called Ena Twigg caused a sensation when it became public knowledge that an American bishop called James Pike had visited her to make contact with his son Jim.

Jim had died a tragic death. After experimenting with psychedelic drugs in San Francisco, in February 1966 he had shot himself in a New York hotel room. Not long after his death,

Bishop Pike and others close to him had begun to experience poltergeist activity in the apartments the bishop shared with his chaplain and secretary. Soon after this the bishop learned of Ena Twigg's reputation as a medium and on their first meeting, she fell into a trance and began to converse with him in the voice of his son. Young Jim spoke openly to his father about his life and death and accepted responsibility for the poltergeist activities, explaining that he had needed to get his father's attention.

For whatever reason, spirits who communicate in this way seem to be able to describe certain events in the future and Jim Pike told his father that he would be with him when he was in Virginia, which he remarked would be very soon. The bishop knew nothing of any trip to Virginia, but on his way home his plane was rerouted and landed at Dulles airfield, which is on the Virginian side of Washington.

The bishop became convinced that Mrs Twigg's mediumship was genuine. As he said in his book *The Other Side*, there were too many exact references to episodes in his son's life and there was no way that the medium could have known so much about that life or reproduced his son's characteristics in her state of trance.

This was not the end of the Bishop Pike case for Ena Twigg, as in August 1969 the bishop and his wife Diane were on holiday in the Israeli wilderness when they became lost and exhausted. The bishop rested in a cave in the desert while his wife went back for help. She was able to reach civilization, but the rescue party could not find the cave she described and it wasn't until 4 September that the bishop was found there dead.

Three days earlier, while sitting in her home in Acton, London, Ena Twigg had felt she had to sit with her husband and friends in a séance. The moment she went into a trance, the bishop came through, described exactly where his body lay and gave certain messages which were to be passed on to his wife. Later, Diane Pike wrote in an article that the medium had given her details regarding her husband and the ordeal they had both come through that no one else could have known. There were also many references to personal things shared only by the couple.

In Ena Twigg's own book, *The Woman Who Shocked the World*, she describes the situation from her point of view and claims that the spirit of the bishop was around her for days after he had gone missing and when no one had found his body she decided to allow him to come through her and communicate his whereabouts for the sake of his poor wife.

Light Minded

No matter what you read or hear about people who make extraordinary claims about trance mediumship, there is nothing better than to witness them in action. While I was learning about mediumship in my development class I met many interesting trance mediums, some of whom were totally deluded. One man who attended the group for a short while was more of a mediumistic impressionist than a trance medium, as he would go through a repertoire of phoney guides from John the Baptist through most of the 12 disciples to a highly exaggerated Jewish-sounding Jesus. After a while Mrs P. gave him his marching orders. Funnily enough, she chose Good Friday to do this.

To experience the worst side of mediumship only makes you appreciate the real thing even more. I am sure that deluded mediums like the man of the many biblical voices produce this nonsense only to gain attention or feel special in some way. In his case, no one else was harmed by his charade. But people who are vulnerable or even gullible have been taken in by mediums who claim to channel famous spirit guides and this is not acceptable. Once a man from the south of England also claimed to be the medium for Jesus and several women in the church he practised in would sit around the so-called master and listen to his wise words, only to find that the alleged spirit was trying to bed them all. Most of these women saw through the ridiculous act of manipulation, but one of them fell for it and eventually left her husband for the sleeping prophet, and the divorce cost her innocent husband a great deal of money, his home and much heartache. I say this to remind people that for every genuine medium there is someone who is just out for all they can get.

The real experience of sitting with a trance medium will lift you to a more spiritual level and create a feeling of lightness of mind. There is a sort of sharing between the spirit world and this world that is difficult to put into words, but can definitely be felt by all who attend such a session.

Of all of the mediums I have witnessed in a trance state, one sticks in my mind and that was a woman who allowed me to experience a spiritual state of mind which will last with me as long as I live. Her name was Laura and she was the best trance medium that I have witnessed in my lifetime.

Although by now I was experiencing short episodes of trance in my development class, Laura helped me to understand the sequence my mind would go through to be raised from human consciousness to a heightened awareness of the spiritual realities. First I learned to clear my mind and just allow any thoughts to pass through without attaching any importance to them. Then I would focus on relaxing my body. At this point I would become aware of how heavy my body had become and how slow and steady my breathing was. By stilling my body and not allowing my mind to hold any mundane or material thoughts, I would feel a sense of lightness of mind which would expand, as if I were the aura or light which surrounded my body. My physical limitations no longer applied and I could open my mind to the idea of making a connection with the higher spirit who was waiting to link with me. It was as if I had to learn to go halfway to meet the spirits, but this way I could sense more about them and train my mind to hold the state for longer periods each time. Also, I had reached a state where my rational mind would not limit me by dissecting and doubting what I was experiencing. From this state of consciousness I could see, hear and feel spirit people just as I had done in childhood and with the same trust I had had as a child.

Being in an altered state of consciousness like this is like being in a body of light which feels limitless. Time and space have no meaning. When you have to come back to our current reality, it feels like coming back through clouds of mist which become denser and thicker until you feel totally connected with the physical world again. I have often thought that if this is anything like the sensations the spirit goes through when the physical body dies, then what is there to fear?

From Darkness Comes Light

Now I have absolutely no problem with this type of experience as I have trained my mind to cope with such things for the past 15 years and I have an understanding of how it works and how it will benefit people. When I was a child, though, such experiences would happen completely at random.

I go back to when I was 16 years old and sitting with my friend Alex in his bedroom, together with another boy who hung around with us at the time. The three of us were listening to records and talking generally about nothing of any great importance when I began to feel as if my body were vibrating. Even though we were teenagers, we weren't smoking anything funny or drinking alcohol. I have to say I had no wish to have a weird trip or experience any form of paranormal activity. What was about to happen could not have been further from my mind.

I looked at my two friends who were sitting cross-legged on the floor opposite me and noticed that they were becoming darker, yet the room around them was becoming brighter. There was a cold feeling coming up from the floor and I began to sense that my friends were staring at me. The whites of their eyes were almost luminous, but their faces had almost vanished into a cloud of darkness.

Alex broke the silence that had fallen over the room by asking if anyone else felt strange. The other boy said he was scared. 'What's going on?' he asked. 'Everything's got dark.'

The vibrating around me had now grown to such a pitch that my body felt as if it was being shaken, then out of nowhere a voice came from my mouth, saying to Alex, 'I am always with you. Remember, I am always with you, no matter what'. My head was filled with a rushing sound and in a second the room was back to normal.

The three of us just sat staring at each other. Alex was looking directly at my face and I noticed that he was breathing really fast. The other boy asked what had gone on and told me that I was freaky. He got up and left in a hurry, but Alex quietly said to me that he had seen his mother looking at him and speaking to him through my face. Knowing that his mother was dead, I began feel that I had done something wrong, even though I hadn't intended to. I remembered the way my mother would react if I mentioned people that I had seen who were dead. Alex told me not to feel bad about it, as he was all right, and the more he thought about it, the more he smiled.

We sat together for hours that night and I told him about some of the strange things that had happened to me and how people had always said it was wrong even though I had no idea how to make it happen or even how to make it stop. Alex was fascinated and I felt relieved that I had spoken about my bizarre psychic experiences, although at the end of the night, when I had to go home, I asked him not to tell anyone about what had happened or about the things I had mentioned to him.

Somewhere in my twenties I lost touch with my friend, as our lives went in different directions, and I never thought about that strange episode in his house again until one day I was working in a barber shop in Glasgow and to my surprise the boy who had fled the scene came in for a haircut. Now in his thirties, as I was, he asked me if I had heard about Alex. I had no idea what he was talking about. Then he told me that Alex had had a long illness and had died the week previously.

After the initial shock, I remembered the message from Alex's mother and how happy he had been with the knowledge that no matter what, she would always be with him. I look back now and am glad that that message came through, even if I had to experience some strange altered state of consciousness for it to happen. I am sure that when Alex was lying very ill, knowing he was going to die, he would have known that his mother on the other side was waiting for him, no matter what.

When All Around You is in Motion...

Learning about trance mediumship and the process of altering your own state of consciousness to accommodate it is important for any medium. It gives you a much deeper awareness of the mechanics behind mediumship.

Furthermore, the knowledge you gain about yourself and the workings of the human mind also assists you when you are practising your gift with people who come to you in a very emotional state. A medium should know how to still their own mind, no matter how emotional the situation they find themselves in, and this should be made easier by what they have learned in their development about calming their mind and working through their mental problems. It's a bit like emptying out cupboards where we hang on to stuff which we will probably never have any further use for, only in the mind it is about remembering, accepting and then letting go.

If a medium is working from a clear mind, this should help to calm the sitter as well as help the process of giving spirit messages. The aim is to allow the spirit to come through in such a way that the sitter's mind will be raised in its vibration to the level of the medium's mind, which will allow the sitter to feel the spirit energy as well as be given proof of life after death. In a sense a sitting with a trance medium should alter the state of mind of the sitter enough for them to experience a more complete feeling of their loved one. As I often tell people, 'feeling is believing'.

Having gone through such a long training in mediumship, I have not only come to know that there is a spirit world where we will go after physical death, but have also developed my own awareness in the here and now. How I react to situations in my own life has changed somewhat, as instead of reacting emotionally to events which would have at one time upset me, I am able to approach life with a greater level of calmness and acceptance.

Our minds are almost always overactive with worry and fear, and often judgements of people and situations that we have no power over. Such thoughts can cause physical unrest or even illness. One of my spirit teachers would always say, 'When all around you is in motion, be still in your mind and calm the motion'. This is something I hope I have learned to do for myself and maybe even for others too. To look at a situation with calmness of mind usually allows you to see beyond the emotional extremes and realize the underlying cause, which in turn allows you to deal with it in a much more constructive way.

CHAPTER EIGHT

Strands of Time

Strands of Time

As a teenager I often had what I now know were prophetic dreams and visions showing scenes that were about to unfold in my life or that of one of my family or friends. These dreams didn't really mean much to me, as they would often involve simple things like letters arriving that no one expected or sometimes unexpected visits from family members and so on. They would occur when I was waking up – they were the sort of half-awake dreams that people remember having – and in daydreams, when my mind was drifting, normally during maths lessons at school. I got to know the difference between ordinary dreams or daydreams and the prophetic kind, as the latter were always accompanied by a buzzing sound in my head that ended in a pop, and that would snap me out of the contemplative state.

One sunny Saturday afternoon when I was around 10 years old, I was playing with some friends at the back of our house when I suddenly became still, my eyes fixed on the brick wall which ran the length of the lane at the back of the houses in our street. I could hear a breathing sound around my head which became a sort of hum and I felt that I was in a different place but still looking ahead at a brick wall, a much higher wall this time. There were lots of people standing at the foot of the wall, all of them looking up at a young man hanging by one hand and screaming as if he was in pain. Then a fire engine arrived and I could see my father talking with some of the firemen. In a flash the scene changed and I felt that I was moving down a corridor in a hospital and a doctor was standing with my elder brother. With that there was a popping sound and my ears were full of the sounds of my friends playing in the back garden, the vision was over and I immediately went back to playing.

The following day I remember there were lots of children playing in our street ands lots of shouting, screaming and laughter. In the middle of all this, I saw a man running in the direction of my house and I remember watching him knocking on the door. My father came out and I could see the strange man speaking quickly to him and urging him to go somewhere with him. Both men left in a hurry. My father was gone for hours, but returned with my elder brother, whose right arm was in a plaster cast.

My brother had been climbing a wall which was about 30 feet high, looking for birds' eggs. He had put his hand into a hole at the top of the wall where the nest was and his foot had slipped and he had fallen, but his wrist had been trapped and he had been left hanging on the wall. A woman had called for the fire brigade to help him and sent her husband to fetch my father, who said by the time he arrived there was a crowd of people looking up at his son dangling by his hand from the top of a very high wall. Luckily, he escaped with no more than a broken wrist, which was set when my father rushed him off to hospital.

Visions like this occurred throughout my childhood and sometimes I would tell people about them, but more often than not I would keep them to myself, because of the strange reaction I got from people. By the time I had reached my twenties I just accepted that every now and then I would have one of my 'funny turns'. I had no idea what caused them or what to do about them, though I thought that if I could only learn how to work them to my advantage then maybe I could see the outcome of the next race at Epsom. The funny thing is, now I know that it doesn't work like that.

A Collage of Dreams

One of the more bizarre episodes was a dream I had when I was about 23 and working as a hairdresser. That particular morning I woke early. It was a cold winter's morning and I decided that I would stay in bed as long as I could before getting up to face the world outside. My mind became fuzzy and I drifted into that nice state somewhere between sleep and waking. Then I began to hear a soft pulsing sound in my ears like soft breathing, which built up to a buzzing sound. At the same time pictures began to form in my mind of one of the most peculiar scenes imaginable. I could see my father carrying a Dobermann Pinscher to the back of a funeral car, where waiting for him were a vet, a nurse and a motor mechanic. I know it sounds like the start of a joke, doesn't it? However, a popping sound went off in my head and then I was fully awake, but could not get this vision out of my mind. I had no idea at the time that the mish-mash of scenes I had just seen was about to be unravelled by the day's events.

At work I had just finished telling one of my workmates about the strange dream when into the salon came a man who told us that his dog had just been knocked down by a car. Luckily the dog was fine and even more luckily the man driving the car was a vet and he had taken the dog to his surgery immediately for a check-up. Yes, it was a Dobermann Pinscher. The man also told us that his girlfriend had gone with the dog and that she was wearing her nurse's uniform, as she was dressed to go to work.

No sooner had this happened than I had a phone call from my father to tell me that his eldest sister had died and could I come and get him as he had smashed his car on the way to see the funeral director.

My colleague looked at me in total disbelief when she heard what had happened to my father and realized that everything that I had told her earlier had unfolded within a matter of hours, even though my dream had been muddled, a bit of a collage of the day's events.

I'm sure these experiences of second sight have nothing to do with my mediumship, even though as a medium I have been given information about future events in people's lives. When the episodes of second sight occur there is never any feeling of the spirit world around me, I am just aware that I am witnessing something that is outside time. I hear no voices and sense no one, it is a completely visual experience, other than a sound which resembles breathing, which vibrates at a loud, steady, rhythmic pace.

Seers of Tomorrow

I suppose that all of us at one time or another would like to see into our future, particularly when we are stuck at a cross-roads in life – provided, that is, that we could be assured of seeing a favourable outcome, just like the many people who read their horoscopes every day, connecting to the good parts and disregarding the negative. But how certain can we be of the future? Is everything in our life predestined? Or do we have the free will to shape our own destiny?

One thing is for certain: seers, oracles and prophets have been a part of the human race since we first walked this Earth. Some have been heralded as saints while others have been burnt at the stake for heresy. My own experiences of second sight have been random, but it still fascinates me whenever I have a precognitive dream or vision of the future that actually comes true. How does this happen? As with all things relating to the unknown, the best way to gain understanding is to examine the evidence.

Dark Visions

One of the best examples of seership in Scottish history is that of Kenneth Mackenzie, better known as the Brahan Seer, who became known throughout the Highlands in the seventeenth century for his gift of second sight.

The Seer's most famous prediction, which he made just before he was put to death on the orders of the Countess of

Seaforth for alleged witchcraft, was that the long line of Seaforths would end in extinction and sorrow, that the last chief of the line would be deaf and dumb and that although he would have four sons, they would all die before him. The Seaforth lands would then pass from the male line to 'a white-hooded lassie from the East' who would kill her own sister. As signs by which it would be known that these events were about to take place, he described certain physical deformities which would become apparent in four prominent Scottish lairds who would be contemporaries of the last of the Seaforths.

More than 100 years later, the signs started to appear. The deformities were recognized in the four lairds whom the Seer had named. Then Lieutenant-General Lord Francis Humberston Mackenzie, Baron Seaforth of Kintail, former British Governor of Barbados, went deaf after an attack of scarlet fever, and with frightening accuracy, the events foretold in the grim prediction were fulfilled one by one. After the untimely death of the last of his four sons, Lord Seaforth never spoke again. He died deaf and dumb on 11 January 1815 and his estates passed to his eldest surviving daughter, who returned hooded (in widow's weeds) from the East, where her recently deceased husband, Admiral Sir Samuel Hood, had been in command of British naval forces in the East Indies. The last tragic part of the prediction came true when this white-hooded lassie was driving a carriage which was involved in an accident in which her sister, Lady Caroline Mackenzie, was killed.

This is but one of many prophecies attributed to the Brahan Seer which, though inconceivable at the time, have come to pass with astonishing accuracy.

Destiny or Predestiny?

The tragic nature of this tale is typical of many predictions of the future. It also suggests that there is no way to change the future, that certain events may already be predestined. Unlike divination, where the reader is trying to tap into the future using a device or instruments, the person gifted with second sight does not try to make deliberate predictions, but simply sees the future under certain circumstances.

Once while I was in a trance state someone asked my spirit guide if he could predict the future. My guide replied that predicting the future was a 50:50 guess based on the feeling the person making the prediction had at that particular moment. But he then went on to describe a scene in the questioner's near future. Shocked, they asked how he was able to see into the future in such a way. My guide explained that in the spirit world they have a much wider vision of life than we do and a better understanding of probability. Within days his prediction came true.

I believe the gift of second sight differs greatly from that of clairvoyance or mediumship. The tarot reader or crystal gazer offers a reading of an intuitive nature, one that depends upon their ability to gain information about a person psychically, and then, using their own intuition, makes predictions based on their feelings. A medium, on the other hand, must establish a contact with a relative in the spirit world who in certain circumstances may give information regarding forthcoming events. In my experience, such information only comes when the recipient of the spirit message needs reassurance about the future. Either way, this type of 'clear seeing', or clairvoyance, deals with predictions surrounding a person with a need. I would suggest that it is the need which instigates the very predictions that they seek.

Seership of the kind demonstrated by the Brahan Seer reaches much further forward in time and offers no comfort or guidance. Also, the Seer needed no personal contact with the people involved. This type of prediction is further illustrated by Nostradamus, who gave accurate descriptions of certain events that took place during the French Revolution, even though he lived more than 200 years previously.

So there may be a difference in the ways in which people can see into the future and how far they can see. If we accept, however, that even one person has truly seen future events, then we are left to ponder the nature of time itself.

The Window of Time

When someone tells you about an event that will happen in your life that you cannot even imagine yourself and then it comes true, all you can think is 'How did they know that?'. Is there some gap that appears in time that people can see through? Some of the forecasts given to me in my life certainly make me think so.

When I was a child my parents encountered a woman who described my future life to them, saying that I would become well known as a clairvoyant and would demonstrate my gift in many places around the world. This has already happened, although at the time neither my parents nor I even understood what a clairvoyant did.

Then, on entering a Spiritualist church for the first time in my early twenties, at the request of a good friend, I was singled out by the medium and told that in five years' time I would stand in that very church and do what the medium was doing. It was indeed five years later, almost to the day, that I gave one of my first demonstrations of clairvoyance in public.

When my good friend and fellow medium Albert Best told me that he had a vision that I would work in Japan, but not in his lifetime, I took no notice of him. But one year after Albert passed to the spirit world, I gave a public demonstration of mediumship in Tokyo.

My friend Dronma, who is a psychic artist, turned to me one evening, sketch pad in hand, and showed me a drawing of a Springer Spaniel dog. 'This dog is for you, Gordon,' she said. 'I saw him sitting at your door and drew him for you.' Nine months later a friend asked if I would take a dog that needed a home. I went to see this dog, only to find out that it was a Springer Spaniel. On his kennel papers was his date of birth: 9 December 1995 – the very day that Dronma had drawn him for me.

This sort of thing has happened to me many times – far more often than coincidence would suggest – not to mention the many times I have made predictions for others and later found that they have come true. Looking back at all of these experiences, I have tried to understand how it works.

The Force is with You

The more I consider the number of random episodes of second sight that happen to people when they least expect it, the more I see that we live as people in time and space, but there must be a part of our consciousness which exists outside time.

A story told by Sir Alec Guinness comes to mind. Sir Alec had just spent many hours on a plane to New York and was feeling exhausted and hungry. He and his agent had already tried many restaurants without finding a free table when they entered a small Italian bistro. Once again they were told that there were no tables available. Sir Alec was almost ready to give up and return to his hotel for much-needed sleep when James Dean got up and kindly asked them to share his table. Before they sat down, Dean asked if they would step outside the restaurant for a second, as he had something he would like them both to see.

Outside was a sports car which James Dean told them he had just bought. He was very excited about it. Strangely, instead of congratulating him, Sir Alec said, in a voice he could hardly recognize, 'Please never get in it. If you get in that car, you will be found dead in it by this time next week'. The time was 10 o'clock, Friday 23 September 1955. The following Friday at 4 a.m. James Dean was found dead in the smashed car.

Alec Guinness claimed never to have done anything like this before in his life and to have no idea how or why it happened to him. Remember, this happened before he found the force in the *Star Wars* movie! My feeling is that it was to do with his state of mind at the time, that his tiredness opened his mind to a line of time concerning James Dean and the car. Most episodes of precognition occur when the mind is drifting between sleep and waking.

Truths and Misconceptions about Second Sight

- *Little old ladies who live in caravans can see into your future.* Some can, but seers can also wear business suits and Cartier jewellery and drive BMWs.
- *Anyone calling themselves a clairvoyant can give an accurate description of your future at will.* This isn't the case – more often than not the genuine phenomenon is a random occurrence.
- *Seers can see everything about you by just looking at you.* No, this isn't true, so the skeletons in your closet are quite safe!
- *Certain items, like crystal balls, stones or cards, will predict future events.* These are merely props which

the seer focuses on. The real predictions come from within the seer's mind.

- *Second sight is always considered a gift.* To some who really possess it, it is a curse, as some of what they see may not be pleasant.
- *Always consult a clairvoyant before you get married.* Honestly, if you have to ask a clairvoyant this, the answer is no!

Seeing Down Under

Is second sight a natural faculty that is latent in everyone and is brought to the fore when conditions are suitable for it to operate? I ask this because of the number of accounts I have heard from people who don't consider themselves to be psychic yet have seen events before they have taken place.

An example of this came from a customer in a hairdressing salon where I worked in the mid-1980s. While having her hair set in perm rollers, Mrs Grove began to relate the story of how earlier that week she had had a very peculiar experience. It was the kind of tale that forced everyone to take notice. She started by saying how she had been thinking of her daughter who was studying at a university in the north of Scotland when she had fallen asleep in her chair, only to find her mind beginning to wander in a dreamlike state. She found herself standing on top of the opera house in Sydney, looking down at the harbour, where she could see her daughter and a young man sitting having a drink and laughing. The moment that she began to question her dream, it ended and she became fully awake again. By now all of the staff in the salon were tuned into the story and waiting to hear what was so strange about it.

Our customer shared the second part of the story with us as she was moved to sit under the hairdryer. Two days after her dream her daughter phoned to tell her she was taking the next year out of her studies and was going with a friend to Australia for a break.

Mrs Grove said she had never experienced anything like it before in her life and had no explanation for how it could have happened. Incidentally, her perm turned out fine, but then I'd seen that coming!

This may not be the most outstanding premonition, but to our customer it really was amazing. As with most episodes of second sight, the seer was looking into a time that she didn't understand, because it was out of time with her life. In this case, her daughter had already made her decision, so her future had been shaped and plans had been put into action, but her mother was unaware of it. It is this type of experience that leads me to believe that those who see events before they happen actually experience them in a state of consciousness that is out of normal time.

I also feel that prophets and seers receive their visions when their minds are affected by certain emotional states, either their own or those of people around them. We only have to look at the Brahan Seer's last prophecy to have some indication of this, as he was about to be burned at the stake at the time. Imagine his feelings towards the family who had deemed him a witch and were now putting him to death. Was it because of the power of his emotions that he could see so far into the future and see the downfall of the family?

For the likes of Mrs Grove, there is not the same emotional intensity, yet the emotion is still there. Her concern for her daughter's future led her mind to drift to a place in her child's life where she saw happiness for her.

I believe that most cases of second sight are born out of human emotion, from prophets like Nostradamus to the fortune tellers with their cards and crystals, remembering that most people who seek advice about the future do so because they are in the middle of some kind of dilemma or other.

Karmic Probability

An explanation that sits well with me is that predictions come from what I call 'karmic probability'. This is when we have taken a decision or carried out an action which will steer us towards a particular point in our life.

It is also my belief that most of our lives are in fact mapped out for us, but that they are made up of many paths that reach out before us like strands of thread running through time, which allows us a certain amount of free will in our lives. Where some of these strands may connect to our own future, others will reach further in time, affecting events long after we are gone. The free will that people exercise in their lives is seen when the strands of time cross to form a junction, leaving a person to choose which thread to follow, much like standing in a train station and deciding how best to carry on your journey. People who have seen visions of the future have tapped into certain strands of time and seen particular junctions in a person's future or even the future of generations to come.

I believe that everyone has this faculty. Even though it may be latent most of the time, it can come into play if the conditions are right. The feeling of knowing that something is about to happen, which I am sure most people have experienced at some point in their lives, is the first indication of this happening, but the majority of people dismiss such thoughts or put them down to coincidence. If they would only consider how many amazing accounts there are of second sight and how many people have experienced it right here and now, they might think differently about the subject.

Time is far from being fully understood, even though physics has come so far. Are there subtle dimensions within time itself and how much of human consciousness is present in time? How do certain people manage to see through time? The mechanics are as yet little understood, but what we do know is that such phenomena operate within certain boundaries and limitations. The seer cannot see everything.

It is quite obvious to me that with our current knowledge of physics, we will not be able to even begin to approach this subject in the way we need to. However, having said that, at the rate at which human consciousness is developing, I would say that it is *only a matter of time*.

CHAPTER NINE

Reincarnation

Reincarnation

As I have said, I've had my fair share of strange happenings in my life and many of them occurred when I was young and had no real way of understanding what I was experiencing.

The night before my sixteenth birthday I was spending time in London with my Aunt Sylvia and Uncle Mick. My uncle had been trying to surprise me by booking a day trip to Paris as a birthday present, but was finding it difficult to get tickets at such short notice. Even as I got ready for bed the night before, no one had breathed a word to me about the surprise.

In the early hours of the morning I got up to go to the bathroom and when I returned to bed I began to have the most vivid dream. I seemed to be falling, although it wasn't like the dreams I usually had of falling fast towards the ground and waking just before I crashed into the earth. In this case I was falling backwards, tumbling gently round and round. Then in a second I was upright and moving forward in a sort of light until I passed right through a wall and found myself in a bar. The people in the bar looked as if they were in a film, as their clothes belonged to the Second World War. The men were in military uniforms and women were in knee-length skirts, some wearing scarves on their heads, others with their hair rolled up at the back and waved on top, typical of the 1940s.

Their voices at first sounded like a babble until as if by magic, there was an adjustment to the sound and I could hear some people speaking French and others speaking English, some with American accents. At first I seemed to be walking around undetected and then I noticed that someone was holding my hand and leading me through the crowded bar towards the far end, where some stairs led up to another level. I remember thinking to myself, *Where am I?* Then I heard a voice in the bar say, 'Dieppe'. I was none the wiser, as I had never heard of Dieppe in my life.

The dream ended in an abrupt manner when the hand which seemed to be leading me pulled me so that I turned round and I was looking in a mirror at two people holding hands, a young man in an airforce uniform and a blonde girl of about the same age. They were looking back at me in the mirror. Then suddenly they both magnified in size and advanced towards me until I felt the woman walk right through me. This made my head burst with an almighty sound that shot me out of the dream and I found myself sitting up in bed.

I never mentioned the dream to my aunt or uncle in the morning as I had forgotten all about it as soon as my aunt had come in and wished me happy birthday and told me I must get up soon as they had a surprise for me. I was told that I was being taken to France for the day by my uncle, but we would have to leave very soon to drive to the coast and catch the ferry. It turned out my uncle had been unable to book the trip to Paris, but instead had decided to take me to Boulogne.

I remember being so excited – until, that is, we reached the dock and were told that we had missed the morning trip and would have to wait until the afternoon for the next one. My uncle was very disappointed and was about to come up with some new idea for a birthday treat when a man at the dock came over and told him that if we could drive down the coast to Newhaven, we might still catch the boat across to Dieppe.

When I heard the word 'Dieppe' something inside me exploded and my heart almost stopped. My uncle asked me if I was all right, but I said nothing to him of my inner feelings as we ran to the car and sped off along the coast. Somehow we managed to reach the boat on time and quickly settled down for the crossing. I had never been out of the UK in my life and I couldn't wait to get to France just so that when I got back to Scotland I could tell my brothers I had been to a foreign country.

Arriving at the port in Dieppe turned out to be the strangest experience, as my uncle said we should find somewhere nice to go and have lunch and I replied, 'Well, we are going in the wrong direction. The best cafés are up to the right'. Mick looked at me in a very strange way indeed, but followed my lead. I really did know the place somehow and soon I had led us to a very chic café, which turned out to be exactly the same as the one in the dream I had had hours earlier. When I noticed the stairs leading to the upper level, I told my uncle that I had to go and look in the large mirror at the top. It wasn't visible from where we were standing, but when I got to the top of the stairs, there it was.

Sitting in that café made me feel so overwhelmingly sad and I kept remembering places and events which somehow belonged to me and yet how could they? Faces would flash up in my mind, names, the sound of voices. Just as in the dream, different languages and accents were all running around in my mind and I felt happy and sad in turn, as if a life were flashing before me. Mick asked me why I had gone so quiet and it dawned on me that this was my birthday and I was supposed to be happy, I had to clear my mind of this stuff.

We left the café soon after and were shopping for gifts for my mother and aunt when again Mick suggested a certain route and I told him no, as there was only a church down that road. Again he gave me an odd look. We walked round the corner and there it was, the old church, just as I had said. This sort of thing happened for the rest of the day and I had no idea why I remembered so much about a place I had never been to before. Even at that age I had already experienced episodes of mediumship and had picked up psychic messages for other people, but this was very different. It was just like remembering.

I felt exhausted when we got back on the boat and I slept all the way back to England and then again in the car to London and right on through the night. The following morning I woke feeling wonderful, refreshed, somehow lighter.

I think of what happened in Dieppe whenever I am asked about reincarnation. To this day this is the only experience that I have had which may or may not have been some kind of past-life memory. I am still not sure, but having looked at the subject now for many years, and hopefully with an open mind, it would seem to me that there are too many supporting cases coming to light for past-life memories to all be coincidence.

Living with the Past

The idea of reincarnation has been around for thousands of years. It was an accepted part of Christianity until the sixth century, when the Roman Emperor Justinian threw the weight of his support behind an opposing doctrine. After that, anyone found preaching reincarnation would be excommunicated. It wasn't until the thirteenth century that the idea appeared again among the Christian sect known as the Cathars. The Catholic Church directed a crusade against them, killing hundreds of thousands of people in the Languedoc region of France. Is it any wonder that the Catholic soldiers were reluctant to accept reincarnation, which according to Eastern religions works on the basis of taking responsibility for your own actions?

The idea has, however, been examined more carefully in recent times. Perhaps one of the best known of the current researchers into the subject is Doctor Ian Stevenson. To date he has investigated several thousand cases of children who have spontaneously recalled previous lives. Dr Stevenson's methodology is sound and he has developed many techniques which enable him to check if the child could have learned the so-called memories through ordinary means and to check out the details of the past life.

Some of the children have been able to pinpoint exact streets and houses from their past lives, even though they were in places these children had never been to in this life. Some have been able to talk to people from their past lives in a way unique to the dead person they were claiming to be. Dr Stevenson also found that many of the children who remembered a past life would be born in this life with a scar or birthmark relating to suffering in the former life.

Healing Old Scars

Carol Bowman's book *Children's Past Lives* also gives many accounts of children who remembered former lives. For Carol her first encounter with this happened when her 5-year-old son Chase suddenly developed an unexplainable fear of fireworks. Some time later that year a hypnotherapist happened to be visiting her and she told him about it. He had experience in past-life hypnotic regression with adults and asked if he could try something similar with the boy.

With no need for hypnotic induction, Carol's son responded to questions put to him by the therapist and recalled being a soldier carrying a gun, which he described as having a sword on the end of it. Then he described a pain in his wrist, which in this life had been affected by eczema ever since he was a baby. In the past life he remembered flashing lights of gunfire around him and being shot in the wrist. Within a few days of the recall experience his eczema completely disappeared, as did his fear of fireworks.

Adults can also be helped by past-life therapy. In his book *Many Lives, Many Masters*, Dr Brian Weiss relates the case of a young patient of his called Catherine, who had been suffering nightmares and chronic anxiety attacks. After treating her with all the traditional forms of medicine, Dr Weiss turned to hypnosis and during the sessions he was astonished as Catherine began to relive past-life traumas which seemed to hold the key to her present problems.

While in a hypnotic trance, Catherine was able to give accurate descriptions of her previous lives and the traumas she had suffered in them which linked to her fears in this life. This was amazing enough, but in certain sessions she would arrive at a between-life stage and channel information from spirits of a much higher consciousness, who would give the doctor more information about his patient and even mention details about his own life which no one else was aware of.

Most fascinating was the effect that past-life memories were having on the patient. One of her biggest fears was water, specifically choking on it, to the extent that she could not take pills for fear of choking to death. During one session she remembered a life from 1800 BC where she had been drowning and had eventually choked to death on the water. After this session her fear of water lessened considerably and in no time she was cured of it altogether.

In a short space of time Catherine underwent many hypnotic sessions where she remembered many different lives and the difficulties she had endured in them. Each episode allowed her to cast off more of her present anxiety. In one session, the doctor asked his patient if she could tell him how many times she had lived on this Earth. She replied, 'Eighty-six'. The doctor then asked why she had only tapped into 12 of those and was told by the entranced Catherine that these were the only ones that needed to be concluded. The other 70-odd had no bearing on where she was now.

If all this is seen as evidence that we have lived before, then we must think that we will live again. And as long as serious men and women of science continue their studies into past-life recall, then at some point we may find a way of knowing more about who we once were and how that is affecting who we are now.

Blasts from the Past

The sad thing about this subject is that it is often abused by the deluded and psychic vultures who prey on people who have emotional needs.

It was at a seminar in Germany around 1997 that I encountered a woman who was giving talks and personal sessions of past-life regression. At first I thought nothing of it until about halfway through the week I overheard one of the people who were attending the course comment that she had been told by the past-life woman that she was Mary Queen of Scots in her previous life. I smiled to myself and thought, *Not another one of those*. It always seems to be famous people who come up in past-life stuff – a bit like mediums who insist on having spirit guides like Jesus or St Peter or Confucius. Why not Joe who was a street cleaner in 1900 or something?

As we came to the end of the week, it turned out that masses of people attending the seminar had had past-life life sessions with the woman at £50 per head and all of those I encountered had been told about their famous past life as Joan of Arc or Henry VIII or any other kings and queens from European history. Oh, the odd woman was told of a life of prostitution, but I'm sure the past-life woman only did this to spite the prettier ones on the seminar! It was unbelievable that so many people bought into this scam. I had to go and see the woman, just out of curiosity!

She began by telling me that I was psychic – not bad, considering she had watched me give a demonstration of mediumship earlier in the week. Then she asked if I had any health problems. I told her that my left eye sometimes got infected and she told me that she was seeing me on a ship at the Battle of Trafalgar and that I was Admiral Nelson! 'Didn't he lose his *right eye*?' I said. She looked very cross that I would question her and told me to be quiet and wait, as the visions were changing. After about half a minute of saying, 'Ah yes, ah yes,' to herself, she told me that I had been a prostitute, and not a very high-class one at that. I asked her where she was getting her information from and she replied, 'The Masters'. I assumed that was the name of the bank or building society where she invested all of her money!

Truths and Misconceptions about Reincarnation

- *Dreams of people and places from the past mean you are revisiting a past life*. Not necessarily. Chances are that you have acquired these visions from a book, conversation or movie. Think about it!
- *Everybody was someone famous in their past lives*. Darling, we can't all have been Cleopatra!
- *Exotic past lives make you more interesting*. If you really can remember a past life, then you are probably repeating mistakes from that life and

the memory is a warning to tie up the loose ends
and get on with this life.

- *Who you were in a past life is more important than who
  you are now*. All you are now is an accumulation of
  all you have been.

- *If you are bad in this life, you may come back as an
  animal*. Actually, some animals are more enlightened
  than humans.

- *Being successful in this life guarantees success in the
  next*. No, in a future life you may have to face
  more difficult times in order for your consciousness to expand.

Nations Remember

To understand past-life memories and the effects they may
be having on the here and now, you first have to accept the existence
of consciousness. The Dalai Lama, spiritual leader of Tibet, says in
his book *The Way to Freedom*:

> If we come to understand that the
> continuity of the consciousness cannot be exhausted

in one lifetime, we will find that there is logical support for the possibility of life after death. If we are not convinced of the continuity of consciousness, at least we know that there is no evidence that can disprove the theory of life after death. We cannot prove it, but we cannot disprove it. There are many cases of people remembering their past lives vividly. It is not a phenomenon confined to Buddhists. There are people with such memories whose parents do not believe in life after death or past lives. I know of three cases of children who have been able to remember their past lives vividly. In one case the recollection of the past life was so vivid that even though the parents previously did not believe in life after death, as a result of the clarity of their child's recollections, they are now convinced.

I do believe that many of us are influenced by past emotional experiences, whether we remember them or not, which still have an impact on the present. I have come to learn that places, too, hold memories of past events. Traumatic events like wars and massacres, I'm certain, leave a stain in the consciousness of a place or even country or continent which can be picked up by the people living there. Just as ghosts are emotional stains left imprinted on time and space, so too a nation can have emotional stains imprinted on the consciousness of that place.

A Spirit World or a World of Spirit?

Back in 1997 I was working as a tutor at the Arthur Findlay College for Psychic Studies when one afternoon I noticed there was to be a lecture on reincarnation by two men, one the editor of *Reincarnation* magazine and the other from the College of Psychic Studies in London. As the subject always raises great debate among Spiritualists, I thought it would be interesting to go along and listen.

In the rather grand library room about 80 people were crammed into every available seat to listen to the lecture. The man from the college spoke clearly about consciousness and energy and used a scientific approach, whereas the editor talked more about the religious side of reincarnation and the law of cause and effect. The intensity in the room was growing as I could feel the people in the crowd anxious to ask questions. When the time came to do so, it was an absolute bunfight. Almost every hand rose in the air at once. The first and most expected question had to be: 'If we reincarnate, then who are mediums contacting in the spirit world?'.

The man from the College for Psychic Studies explained that consciousness had many layers and said that the physical form was only a small part of the overall energy field of an individual consciousness. At death a person's spirit returned to its overall higher consciousness with memories of its recent life, yet the higher consciousness could also project spirit energy into a new physical life at the same time.

If this is true, then it would have to mean that one consciousness could give life to many people at the same time. This can be linked to the idea of a soul group, where many people are working from the same higher consciousness at the same time and each one has come into the material world with the same goal or purpose.

Many other questions were asked that day, like what time span was involved between each rebirth and why did we need to live so many lives in the physical world and who decided if we should reincarnate. The answers given pleased some people, but not all, yet at the end of the lecture we were asked to put up our hands if we believed in reincarnation and I was quite surprised to see that at least 90 percent of the people in that room raised their hands. About the same number again admitted to feeling that this was not their first life on Earth.

It was that day, just after that lecture, that I began to think about consciousness being more universal than each individual person. I wondered what was really beyond death. I know I had seen, heard and sensed spirits all my life and I had been given messages from spirits that were very accurate and had helped many people through their bereavement, but was that all there was to the human spirit? And what about the spirit world, was it just an in-between stage where spirit adjusted before moving on to the next level? Or could it be that we are living in a world of spirit right now in our human form and we don't even recognize it, so we have to come tumbling back for life after life until we can understand it all?

When I left the Arthur Findlay College at the end of the week I knew that I had to look more deeply into the subject.

The Meaning of Life and Life and Life

Since 1997 I have studied the religions that believe in reincarnation and the scientific studies into the subject. As well as this, I have listened to many people's accounts of past-life recall. The one thing that comes to my mind whenever I think of people who remember a previous life is *Why?* Why are memories, almost always traumatic memories, still haunting the mind in its new incarnation?

I believe it can only be that there is unfinished business. I know it is the people who die unexpectedly and have unfinished business in this life who communicate best through a medium. Their intention is always to tie up all the loose ends so that they can move on spiritually. It may be that the past-life episodes that are remembered are those that need to be healed in order to allow progression of the human spirit. This would explain the findings of people like Dr Brian Weiss.

If we have lived many lives in many countries and different cultures, it may also be that when we revisit these places some memory is triggered. This may have been what happened to me in Dieppe, only the visions appeared prior to my being told I was going there – unless such episodes can be perceived by the unconscious mind ahead of time?

I go back to what the Dalai Lama says: 'To understand the nature of rebirth, you first have to understand consciousness.' I look at consciousness as being like the hard drive of a computer which has masses of memory, so even when one program is being run on the screen there are still many available on the hard drive, some of which have been run before and some of which will be run in the future. By looking at consciousness in this way,

I can see that as a medium, even when I am using one program, I can still access files from other programs. So the memories of a person who has died can be accessed from their consciousness databanks and relayed back to their loved ones, even if they have now reincarnated into another body. In this sense mediumship is the ability to tap into the spiritual hard drive.

When I look at things in this way I have no problem in understanding that we have a greater consciousness, the main computer if you like, which houses all that we have ever done in all our lives. Past-life memory might then interfere with our current program, or life, along the lines of a fault which would have to be put right in order for our current program to run smoothly.

The thing about reincarnation is that it is a system of refining life actions and learning from mistakes. It encourages those who believe in it to take responsibility for all their actions so as to create good karma and allow their consciousness to expand and grow. Otherwise, you will only repeat the same lessons until you have learned them.

What makes this idea sometimes difficult to accept is our natural human emotions. These often blind us to the bigger picture and close our minds so that we think that all we are is a person who may or may not have lived before and who may or may not live again.

Because of what I have experienced in my life as a medium, I know that I am more than this. I know that though my physical body will die one day, I will not. I know that my spirit will learn from all that I have experienced in this life as Gordon Smith and will add that program to the memory in my spiritual databank. My next program might run in a more subtle spirit world of light or it may run back here on Earth. I don't have the words to describe the stages I will go through after death, but one thing I can say is that I am conscious of living now, and that is most important.

CHAPTER TEN

Consciousness

Consciousness

Trying to understand ourselves is not easy. We must be one of the greatest mysteries known to man. Are we humans who will live in a spirit world after we die or are we spirits living a human life?

Questions like these and many more were running through my mind while I was driving to the countryside back in 1992, during a time in my life when I felt cut off from everything and everyone. It was one of those times when nothing seems to make sense, the kind of experience that most of us go through when we feel that the world is coming in on us and we just need a reality check. I was driving my car that day without really concentrating on where I was going and my mind was clouded with thoughts of *What's it all about?* and *There's got to be more to life than this.* Let's face it, I was having a bad hair day!

I pulled my car onto a grass verge at the side of the road in the Campsie Glen, a quiet place not more than a half-hour's drive to the north of Glasgow. I often went there to escape from the world. Its beautiful hills, glens and waterfalls cascading through rugged ravines were always a welcoming sight. The hills were not alive with the sound of music that day, in fact they were empty of people, which was just what I wanted. I had to get away from the city and all of the people who were in my life and all of the thoughts which were clouding my mind.

I felt as though I had every worry of the world on my shoulders: the end of my marriage, thoughts of my children, uncertainty about what I was doing in my life as a medium. I just didn't feel that I had any foundation, and more than that, I didn't have a clue what was real and what wasn't. I sat alone at the side of a large waterfall, my head slumped, and asked out loud: 'What am I all about?'. I remember taking a deep breath and trying to meditate, but all I wanted to do was cry. So many material problems rushed through my mind at once and again I thought, *What am I all about?* Then I just sat for some time listening to the roar of the waterfall, the sound rushing through me until I felt it had almost become part of my thinking.

Suddenly I became aware of the sound of a branch creaking in the distance and of the tiny trickle of water some 10 feet from where I was sitting. It was as if someone had turned the waterfall off and yet they hadn't. Without lifting my head I knew which tree I could hear the creaking sound from and not only was I aware of the trickling stream, but without looking I could describe every stone that the water was rippling over. I was seeing every blade of grass around me individually, yet without looking at any of them. A sense of calm ran through me like nothing I had ever felt before in my life. Suddenly I was alive – awake to the life around me and the life that was in me. I felt connected to everything that was alive. Every living thing was a part of me and I was a part of it.

This was one of the most amazing feelings that I had ever experienced, greater than seeing spirits or watching inanimate objects fly around a room. I was conscious of life, not phenomena. I *felt* alive, as if this was the real me – a me that had always existed, but had never been able to come to the surface. All of the times when I had tried to meditate and thought that I had achieved a state of spiritual ecstasy simply paled by comparison. My mind had expanded until I seemed to be way beyond my physical body, but I was not having an out-of-body experience or in a state of trance that I could associate with discarnate spirits. This was the real deal – my spirit was in touch with all the life around me. This was the first time I had felt what it was like to be consciously aware of life. It was mind-blowing.

I left the glen on the most amazing high. All at once I had gained an understanding of myself that I had never had before, even though I had seen and sensed things that many people could not understand. But now I was aware of myself as a spirit in the material world.

From that moment on I felt compelled to investigate my own spirit in the same way that I had looked into life after death in order to help others. I needed to know the truth, as I knew it would help people to understand more about the nature of life and death and about consciousness itself.

Fear and Limitation

For years I had witnessed visions and heard voices of spirits and on the evidence I had given people through my mediumship, I knew that there was a life after physical death. But the overwhelming feeling I had just experienced gave me a much wider view of the human spirit. It made my belief much more concrete. More than that, I began to look at life in a completely different way. I could see how in spirit form we have a greater connection to all life and much broader vision, which is why spirits on the other side can give us information about future events and answers to problems which seem insurmountable to us in our limited human state. I could understand how consciousness is capable of producing phenomena that the human mind can't explain. I could understand how a mind which has experienced even a moment of expansion becomes more accepting of the so-called supernatural.

My experience was just a glimpse, I'm sure, of what our minds are capable of when not restricted by our emotions.. The concerns and worries which we experience in this life are the limiting force which stops us from accepting what we are capable of at our best. Fear is the root which keeps the human mind earthbound. Yet there is so much for us to tap into and grow towards if we can only allow ourselves to become less limited in our thinking.

Many people of today tend to live inside their head. Their whole world is governed by their thoughts and many of those thoughts become fears and anxieties, worries about not having enough material goods or what others will think, fears of losing a loved one or losing themselves. This type of thinking keeps the mind running round and round like a wheel, never expanding, but repeating patterns of limited fearful thoughts which the mind then becomes accustomed to and cannot let go of.

A story told to me by a Buddhist monk is a prime example of how some people will never let go of their concerns. The monk was repeating a story he had overheard about two monks who had taken a vow of celibacy. This vow forbade them to have any contact with women, to the point where they were not even allowed to shake hands. One morning the two monks were returning to the monastery when they came across a young woman who was stuck halfway across a stream. She looked towards the monks for help, but knowing the order they came from, realized that she could not ask for assistance. Yet one of the monks moved quickly in her direction, lifted her in his arms and carried her to the other side.

After the evening prayers back in the monastery the two monks were sitting together when one turned to the other and said, 'I can't get it out of my head that you carried that young woman across the river this morning'.

The other replied, 'I left her there this morning. You are still carrying her, it would seem'.

Learning to let go of your concerns is the first step in allowing your consciousness to expand. Letting go of fear of situations you cannot change will also gently open up the mind to other levels of consciousness.

Truths and Misconceptions about Consciousness

- *The human brain is our consciousness.* Not so – all that we are is consciousness. The brain is just a tiny part of that.
- *Consciousness is only a part of our lives.* The reality is that our lives are only a part of consciousness.

- *Consciousness is limited by time and space.* Consciousness is vast and many-layered. Our waking human consciousness, if measured in the scale of things, would be like a tiny grain of sand.

- *Consciousness is fixed and unchanging.* Consciousness is ever changing, ever growing. It's we who seem to be static by comparison.

- *Only humans are conscious.* Consciousness is the life force which runs through the universe. All life is a part of it. To cause harm to anything within it must surely cause harm to yourself.

- *There's no need to explore your own consciousness.* Every living being is driven to expand its own consciousness as part of the greater whole.

The Mind Doctor

The famous psychiatrist Carl Gustav Jung spent many years journeying through his own consciousness. From childhood the Swiss scientist was aware of being two different personalities: one which lived in the outer world and went to school and was more or less the same as many other boys, and one which was more grown up, sceptical and withdrawn from the physical world. Somehow he felt that his second personality, which he described as an inner personality, was more in touch with the beauty of nature and connected to the vast undiscovered universe and everything that lived within it.

Through many years of investigation Jung discovered that this inner 'subconscious' mind was connected to a higher mind which he called 'the collective unconscious' and described as a store of knowledge of all times and events, past, present and future – the hard drive I was talking about earlier. Jung felt that the collective unconscious was the reason for people becoming aware of similar information at the same time, even if they were living in different parts of the globe. Like the subconscious mind, it could communicate with the conscious mind through dreams and in other symbolic ways, including through a series of meaningful coincidences, which he called synchronicity.

I remember such an instance that took place not so long ago in my life. I had ordered some travellers' cheques in pesetas for a forthcoming trip to Spain, but when I went to the bank to pick up the cheques, I noticed that they were in fact in American dollars. The amazing thing was that earlier that morning I had had a phone call from a Spiritualist organization in America asking if I could come and work there the following month. Rather than change the cheques, I exchanged some more money for pesetas. To me this was a prime example of synchronicity.

First Emotion

A big part of my spiritual journey has been an investigation into my inner self, looking at the emotional part of my life in order to find out more about the inner workings of my mind. A bit like Jung, I can remember two different states of mind in my childhood, one which behaved in a childlike and often childish way and a much more mature, thoughtful self which seemed to take note of things happening around me and record each situation before filing it away. I have found that it is this part of my mind which is connected to the psychic and mediumistic side of my nature.

When I first began to study mediumship, I learned it was important to clear the mind so that it could be used like a clear screen for the spirit world to project images onto it. Our conscious mind is often clouded by our traumatic emotional memories. We must learn to release these memories, as they can fester and restrict the consciousness. For a medium, they will also interfere with messages coming in from the spirit world. So I undertook the task of sorting through my mind to try to find out how many of my emotional memories were relevant to me here and now and how much was just junk which was taking up space in my mind.

My first conscious memory goes back to when I was 4 years old. My mother and I were returning from the local shops around mid-morning and had just started walking up the path leading to the front door of our house when I remember a feeling of fear running through me. I often wonder what people's earliest emotional memories are and if they have any bearing on what happens in the life that follows, as most of my adult life I have worked to try and take away fear from people.

By the time my mother and I had reached the front door, this feeling of foreboding had overwhelmed me. Looking back, I'm sure it came from something I sensed in my mother's behaviour. She had a feeling that someone was in the house and hesitated for a moment before opening the door. I remember clearly that she told me to stand still as she opened the door wide and called out that she knew someone was there. Standing in the open doorway, she called out again, saying that she was sending for the police. I can still remember standing there and wondering what was going on, feeling, I suppose, more afraid for my mother than for myself.

It could only have been seconds later that noises could be heard coming from one of the bedrooms in the house. A neighbour heard the commotion and came running down the path to join us just as we caught sight of a young man running off through our back garden and disappearing down the lane at the end. It appeared my mother had disturbed him before he could do much, as when she and the neighbour searched the house they found nothing had be taken or damaged. The only sign that the man had been there was the open window in the bedroom which he had used to enter and leave the house.

It is quite strange to look back and find that this was truly the first time I was aware of experiencing an emotion. To me, this first emotion is an awakening of the mind. It is the consciousness fusing with the physical world, bringing you straight into the reality of this life. The mind of every young child, I feel, drifts in and out of different states of consciousness before it connects fully with this physical life. This is why it is often difficult to recall our early lives in any detail.

Emotional Garbage

One of the most important things I learned when I began to develop my abilities as a medium was meditation. Learning to meditate taught me a great deal about myself. When I first began the practice, even though I found it easy to sit still and breathe well, it still took me some time to come to terms with stilling the thoughts in my mind. This was the most difficult part of the discipline for me to master. The more I would try and empty my mind of thoughts, the more I would find my head filled with sounds and visions. Instead of a still, peaceful visualization of calm and serenity, mine was like the first day of the January sales in London, with memories, dreams and reflections all clambering to get to the forefront of my conscious mind.

As I continued to meditate, I found that I would fall asleep. This was due to the mental exhaustion I experienced trying to keep thoughts out of my mind. I soon learned that the mind has muscles just like the body and if you over-exercise muscles which have not been used much before, then you are bound to feel the effects of over-exertion. As well as falling asleep I would often complain of headaches at the start – again, my aching mind muscles reminding me to pace myself.

After about six months of practising meditation I began to relax and allow my mind to ease into it. I no longer felt in such a hurry to learn, my busy mind had calmed down and I noticed that fewer thoughts were cramming into my head. Even better, I had learned to let them pass through, like clouds blowing in the wind. These thoughts and images were only my emotional garbage. I was learning to let it all go, whereas before I would have held on to it all, as most people do. But it is only when we can let go of all our stored mind rubbish that we can begin to catch a glimpse of our true selves. I often think of this when I am clearing out a cupboard in my house and find things which I have not used for years and probably will never use again. Once I was not ready to cut the ties with the part of my life they came from. Now, gone are the days when I will let them take up space!

Just like clearing out a cupboard, emptying the mind of its clutter creates a feeling of lightness and space. It is the first step towards understanding consciousness.

After about a year of clearing out my emotional mind rubbish I began to notice many changes in my behaviour, both in myself and towards others. I found myself becoming more patient and less likely to react to emotional scenes. Whereas once I would become involved in everybody's dramas without thinking, now I seemed to be more conscious of the underlying reasons for others' emotional outbursts and would be detached and calm in my own responses. I also began to find that I was much less sentimental than I had been all my life. By clearing my mind of old mental garbage I had become much more balanced, and I had become conscious of it. The emotional detachment I was now aware of was something I had to develop further if I were to work as a medium, as I would be no good to anyone if I became immersed in their grief.

Guiding Light

Emptying your mind of the old conditioning is a preparation for reaching the higher, more subtle states of consciousness. It was when I had done this that I began to go into a trance and became more aware of the spirit guides and teachers and higher energies around me. I often wondered if they were actually a part of my own higher mind or separate entities who were able to link with me because I had become more open-minded. It may be a moot point, because at some level of consciousness, everything is one anyway. This became clearer to me when I listened to a tape of a trance session given by one of my spirit guides back in 2001.

During this particular session I had gone into a trance for a group of people at the Spiritualist Association of Great Britain and my main guide, Chi, had come through to talk to the group. One man asked him to explain the nature of consciousness. As you do! Chi's explanation was as follows:

Consciousness is what you are right now. This very moment is as conscious as you are of yourself. The mind in the human state of consciousness is limited and does not like to go beyond what it knows as reality. Anything beyond your understanding of reality can cause you disturbance because your mind wants to dissect any phenomenon and understand it through reason and rationality, but reason and rationality will limit you from understanding the experience itself.

You must remember that consciousness is life and as such is many-levelled. To gain more understanding of such a vast thing you must know where you are in it yourself. As a human being, you are aware of many things which are less conscious and less aware than you are in your world, but cannot fathom that there are other forms of consciousness which are more conscious of themselves and even more aware of where they exist within reality. Even in this moment, as I speak with you through the body of this medium, are you conscious of me as a separate spirit entity or as a higher part of the mind of the medium, or neither? What does your own conscious mind accept of this experience?

The fact is, I am both separate and connected to the mind of the medium, as are you in this moment; the fact that you cannot see me as a person, spirit or in human form does not mean that I do not exist and if I were to appear to you in this room this very moment it would not convince you of my existence either if you were not ready to integrate such a happening into your consciousness.

The nature of consciousness is what you should ponder, as it is expanding just like the universe in all directions without fear of limitation. To know more of yourself in any given moment you must become like nature itself, ever growing and renewing. Life and death are but segments of the entire process.

Chi also talked of the mind in human form being like a small transistor radio, while the bigger consciousness which feeds it with power was like a massive power station and could not connect fully to the small receiver, as so much power would blow it completely. He also mentioned that spiritual teachers like Christ and the Buddha were like adapters who filtered down some of the power and inspired us to grow and try to understand more of the conscious mind.

Crystal Clear

My vision of consciousness has changed over the past few years. I remember when I first set out as a medium I thought that the spirits who communicated through me lived in a very Victorian well-lit spirit world and that they still resembled people and would be waiting there for everyone they loved to cross over. Many years and many communications later, I have a much broader idea of consciousness during this life and the life beyond.

I think it all began to change for me when I had one of my funny dreams. I call them that because at the time they will mean absolutely nothing to me, but much later they will prove to be very significant.

I looked at the little book of dreams that I keep in a cupboard next to my bed and turned the pages back to a dream headed 'The Diamond' and dated 1993. At the top of the page I had made a note: 'Asking about consciousness'. Something I try to do if I remember a very vivid dream is to note what was prominent in my mind prior to having it. This time it had been consciousness. I began to read the description of my dream.

The dream began with my death. I witnessed myself leaving my body, which lay motionless on a bed. I had no awareness of any spirit body or vehicle, just consciousness. In this state I moved into a light where I could just make out the silhouettes of people who appeared to be made of light. This resembled my own idea of the spirit world.

I was lifted high above this world of light and began to notice what looked like crystals. There were millions of these perfectly clear-cut stones, all individual and yet all connected by strands of light. The thin strands of light, I noticed, were also reaching down into the world of light people below, as if connecting them to the masses of crystals. Somehow I had become connected too. I was part of one of the multifaceted stones. It felt as if my 'self' was one of the many facets and yet I knew I was all of the crystal at one and the same time. Well, I said it was a funny dream!

A beam of light passed through my crystal and suddenly it was a collage of holograms, images of people from different times. Some I could recognize by their outfits, others I could not place, but all the time I was experiencing a certain knowing, as if these were my memories.

The dream changed at this point and I was separated from the crystal and moving at very high speed towards something in the distance below me. It was a woman who was working as a medium, only she was inside a crystal and there were lots of people in crystals trying to link to one of the facets which encompassed her. All of the people in crystals, including me, had a strand of golden light connecting them to each other and this also connected us to where I had just come from.

I never got to link with the mind of the medium in my dream. Instead I was pulled back to my body at such a rate that I woke with a start and found that I was sitting up in my bed in a cold sweat, heart pounding.

The Diamond

Not long after my crystal dream I was visiting Dronma, my psychic artist friend who is also a Tibetan Buddhist. When I told her of my experience of being connected to people inside crystals, she produced a series of drawings she had done over several years, some showing people inside crystals all connected to one another and others showing the universe as interconnecting crystals. I could hardly believe it. She told me that this helped her to understand the nature of consciousness.

I have no problem with the idea that all living things are connected and that it is life which connects us, especially after my experience in the Campsie Glen. I also believe that our life force never dies and that Jung's collective unconscious stores everything that has ever occurred. My way of looking at this is that the memories of each life are kept on file, while the life force itself goes on, either in a spirit dimension or back here in the form of another physical life.

If our consciousness is like a diamond, then I feel that one of the purposes of this journey is to polish it and we can do this by learning more about ourselves. I'm also sure that every bad deed in this life will take away some of the lustre from the stone, but every good one will make it sparkle.

So What Now?

When I look over all of the amazing things that have happened in my life and the lives of others, I realize that there is much more to us than meets the eye. So many people throughout history have experienced glimpses of what the human spirit is capable of producing by way of miracles and other phenomena that defy every physical law. I believe that so-called supernatural mysteries have been given to us in order for us to learn more about our supernature, our spirituality, which it is our destiny to encounter.

The more I realize that my life now is but one tiny program running from a vast source of spiritual consciousness, the less worried I am about experiencing everything I can in this short life, for I know that my life will go on and on beyond the change we call death. I am not surprised when I hear of extraordinary events in this world or witness people who display exceptional spiritual gifts and abilities, as I accept that consciousness is developing at different levels in different people and some will ripen sooner than others, but each individual will have their chance to grow when ready. If we open our minds to all things, then we may experience the unbelievable – and find that it's the truth.

Further Reading

Mary Armour, Helen Duncan, *My Living Has Not Been in Vain*, **Pembridge Publishing, 2001**

Carol Bowman, *Children's Past Lives*, **Bantam, 1997**

Gena Brealey with Kay Hunter, *Two Worlds of Helen Duncan*, **Regency Press, 1985**

Erika Cheetham (trans. and ed.), *The Prophecies of Nostradamus*, **Corgi, 1988**

His Holiness the Dalai Lama, *The Way to Freedom*, **Thorsons, 1997**

Dante Alighieri, *The Divine Comedy*, **Oxford Paperbacks, 1998**

Leslie Flint, *Voices in the Dark*, **Two Worlds Publishing, 2000**

Stephen Hawking, *A Brief History of Time*, **Bantam Books, 1998**

Kalu Rinpoche, *Secret Buddhism: Vajrayana Practices*, **ClearPoint Press, 1995**

David Kennedy, *A Venture into Immortality*, **Colin Smyth Ltd, 1973**

Alexander Mackenzie, *The Prophecies of the Brahan Seer*, **Sutherland Press, 1972**

Daniel C. Matt, *God and the Big Bang*, **Jewish Lights Publishing, 1996**

Radmila Moacanin, *The Essence of Jung's Psychology and Tibetan Buddhism: Western and Eastern Paths to the Heart*, **Wisdom Publications, 2003**

Raymond A. Moody Jr, MD, *Life after Life*, **Corgi, 1975**

James Pike, *The Other Side*, **W. H. Allen, 1969**

Archie E. Roy, *A Sense of Something Strange*, **Dog and Bone, 1990**

Archie E. Roy, *Archives of the Mind*, **SNU Publications, 1996**

Brian Weiss, *Many Lives, Many Masters*, **Piatkus Books, 1994**

Colin Wilson, *The Occult*, **Watkins Publishing, 2003**

The Leslie Flint Foundation. *www.leslieflint.com, 15 Broom Hall, Oxshott, Surrey, KT22 0JZ, United Kingdom*

We hope you enjoyed this Hay House book.
If you would like to receive a free catalogue featuring additional
Hay House books and products, or if you would like information
about the Hay Foundation, please contact:

Hay House UK Ltd

Unit 62, Canalot Studios • 222 Kensal Rd • London W10 5BN
Tel: (44) 20 8962 1230; Fax: (44) 20 8962 1239
www.hayhouse.co.uk

***

Published and distributed in the United States of America by:

Hay House, Inc. • PO Box 5100 • Carlsbad, CA 92018-5100
Tel: (1) 760 431 7695 or (800) 654 5126;
Fax: (1) 760 431 6948 or (800) 650 5115
www.hayhouse.com

Published and distributed in Australia by:

Hay House Australia Ltd • 18/36 Ralph St • Alexandria NSW 2015
Tel: (61) 2 9669 4299 • Fax: (61) 2 9669 4144
www.hayhouse.com.au

Published and distributed in the Republic of South Africa by:

Hay House SA (Pty) Ltd • PO Box 990 • Witkoppen 2068
Tel/Fax: (27) 11 706 6612 • orders@psdprom.co.za

Distributed in Canada by:

Raincoast • 9050 Shaughnessy St • Vancouver, BC V6P 6E5
Tel: (1) 604 323 7100 • Fax: (1) 604 323 2600

***

Sign up via the Hay House UK website to receive the Hay House
online newsletter and stay informed about what's going on with
your favourite authors. You'll receive bimonthly announcements
about discounts and offers, special events, product highlights,
free excerpts, giveaways, and more!
www.hayhouse.co.uk